On Guard *for* Religious Liberty

Six Decades of the Baptist Joint Committee

Pam Parry

SMYTH & HELWYS
PUBLISHING, INC.

Macon, Georgia

ISBN 1-57312-090-1

On Guard for Religious Liberty
Six Decades of the Baptist Joint Committee

Pam Parry

Copyright © 1996
Smyth & Helwys Publishing, Inc.
6316 Peake Road
Macon, Georgia 31210-3960
1-800-747-3016

All rights reserved.
Printed in the United States of America.

The paper used in this publication meets the minimum
requirements of American National Standard for Information
Sciences—Permanence of Paper for Printed Library Materials.
ANSI Z39.48–1984

Photos used by permission of the Baptist Joint Committee.

Library of Congress Cataloging-in-Publication

Parry, Pam.
    On guard for religious liberty:
    six decades of the Baptist Joint Committee/
    Pam Parry.
    x + 86 pp.   6" x 9" (15 x 23 cm.)
    Includes bibliographical references.
    ISBN 1-57312-090-1 (alk. paper)
    1. Freedom of religion—United States—History—20th century.
    2. Church and state—United States—History—20th century.
    3. Baptist Joint Committee on Public Affairs—History.
    4. Southern Baptist Convention—History—20th century.
    5. United States—Constitutional law—Amendments—1st.
    I. Title.
    BR516.P29 1996
    323.44'2'08826—dc20   96-31881
                                                      CIP

Contents

Foreword

Religious liberty—I don't think any two words have had a greater effect on our nation. A desire to worship freely was the common strand that bound the earliest colonists. John Bunyan, the seventeenth-century English author of the classic allegory *The Pilgrim's Progress,* yearned for religious liberty; he wrote his novel while in jail. The crime? Preaching the gospel without a license.

Fortunately, I have what John Bunyan lacked: a United States Constitution. I embrace the First Amendment of our Bill of Rights, which protects us from the very persecution endured by John Bunyan in the 1660s–1670s and others throughout the world today. Our Founding Fathers knew that for religious liberty to be guaranteed, individuals must wholly, decisively, and permanently be released from the clenched fist of an abusive State or institutional church.

While the State earns most of our repudiation today, it is not alone in turning its back to religious liberty. The ecclesiastical authority of the institutional church has more than once shown dissenters little of God's mercy, or His love. It was the clenched hand of the established church that drove the famous Baptist Roger Williams into Rhode Island in search of the freedom to worship.

Unlike John Bunyan and Roger Williams, I have come to naturally expect religious liberty, and under our Constitution, it is a freedom each American has the right to demand. But sometimes, however unobtrusively or even unintentionally, there are moments when our religious liberties are put in jeopardy. Therein lies the purpose of the Baptist Joint Committee: struggling to ensure that what so many take for granted is never taken away.

Mark O. Hatfield
United States Senator

Preface

This book is not a comprehensive history of the Baptist Joint Committee (BJC). Rather, it uses the agency's sixtieth anniversary as an occasion to examine the tenuous nature of religious liberty and the importance of its political corollary, church-state separation. The book does not focus on the BJC as an institution but as a manifestation of the value Baptists place on religious freedom and the eternal vigilance needed to preserve it.

Such an analysis could not be more timely. For centuries, the principle has withstood various pressures. But today, absolute and complete religious liberty faces its toughest predator. Ironically, this enemy was once its most ardent defender. Some Baptists, whose ancestors were the greatest champions of the principle, have not only abandoned it but are intent on its destruction.

If not for the colonial dissidents called Baptists, the First Amendment might never have been adopted. But some of today's Baptists are of a different stripe. They are leading the charge to disarm the very religion clauses that James Madison penned at their forebears' insistence. These revisionists have fooled themselves into believing that they can improve the First Amendment. Do modern-day lawmakers really believe they can outdo great thinkers of the Enlightenment, such as Madison and Jefferson? Do today's Baptists think they care more about religious liberty than their ancestors, such as John Leland and Isaac Backus?

More than any other group, Baptists have been defined by the deep religious conviction that no authority—especially a civil one—can stand between individuals and their creator. So why have some Baptists forsaken this distinction? How can those who once propounded the "wall of separation between church and state" now want special privileges from Caesar? And why do they persecute the Baptists who cling to that heritage? The answers to these questions explain why Southern Baptists could help found the BJC in 1936 and then turn around decades later to besiege and ultimately defund it. The answers also shed light on why prominent Baptist legislators are among those championing a revision of the First Amendment.

The purpose of this book is threefold. First, it will show the pivotal role of the BJC in the adoption of two landmark laws: the Equal Access Act of 1984 and the Religious Freedom Restoration

Act of 1993. Both legislative battles indicate that liberty can never be assumed. They also demonstrate the agency's continued viability in the nation's capital. Second, it will explore the unholy matrimony of politics and religion that has tainted the largest Protestant denomination in America, the Southern Baptist Convention (SBC). Third, the book will discuss the SBC's vendetta against the BJC. Unable to control the agency, the denomination unsuccessfully sought to stamp it out of existence. The evidence clearly indicates that the SBC, not the BJC, changed its position on church-state separation.

Given the stated purpose, I must concede the book's limitation. I am biased. I believe fervently that the principle of religious liberty is revealed in the nature of Jesus Christ. I also believe that the best way to ensure religious freedom is to separate religious and civil authority. That makes me an unapologetic supporter of the BJC—a conviction that predated my employment there. So up front, I must admit that this book will represent one point of view. But, that limitation is also the book's strength. Who better to write of Baptists' commitment to a principle than someone who has staked reputation and career on its endurance?

Acknowledgments

Several people helped bring this book to life—probably more than I should attempt to name—but some friends deserve particular recognition.

First, a special thanks to reporters who helped to ensure an accurate, reliable record of Baptist life during a tumultuous time. Baptist Press and Associated Baptist Press articles were among the many resources used for this book. Special thanks to W. C. Fields, Al Shackleford, Dan Martin, and Marv Knox for their leadership at a time when journalistic ethics and professionalism were not only scarce but shunned by their bosses. Also, kudos to Greg Warner and Bob Allen for continuing the legacy of integrity after Baptist Press was dismantled as a reliable news source. Thanks for your skills as newsmen and for your witness.

Second, the former and current staff of the Baptist Joint Committee have given tremendous input. Thanks to all, particularly Dan Age, Charline Berry, Rosemary Brevard, Kenny Byrd, Larry Chesser, James M. Dunn, Jeannette Holt, Joyce Johnson, Quentin Lockwood III, Gary McNeil, Karen McGuire, Melissa Rogers, Oliver S. Thomas, and J. Brent Walker. Dan Age and Melissa Rogers kept the writer on track during the initial stages of the project. Rosemary Brevard reviewed the first draft and improved the manuscript. Gary McNeil gave background for the equal access chapter. To all, thanks for your insights.

And a special thanks to Stan Hastey for granting permission to use his doctoral dissertation on the history of the Baptist Joint Committee, published October 1973, as the basis of chapters 2 and 3. His scholarship and generosity enriched this product. Also helpful were the personal papers of Rufus W. Weaver, used in chapter 2, and the master's thesis of Dorothy Cherry Schleicher, published December 1993, used in chapter 3.

To our friends who put principle above politics to ensure the Baptist Joint Committee's viability into the next century.

Chapter 1
Freedom's Roots

"Conscience is the most sacred of all property."
—James Madison

What the Babe did for baseball, Baptists did for American democracy. Neither conceived their institutions, but both helped make them what they are today. The difference? Virtually every American knows of Ruth's legendary prowess as the game's longtime home-run king. His escapades are part of American folklore. Tragically, about the same number of citizens do not have a clue how much they owe their civil liberties to a dissident group known as Baptists.

While Baptists did not singlehandedly secure democracy in the New World, they made a contribution without which the new experiment in governing would have been hollowed. That contribution? Absolute and complete religious liberty for all citizens. Without that principle safeguarded, other liberties could be imperiled.

Most Americans identify Thomas Jefferson and James Madison with the First Amendment—which guarantees freedom of religion, speech, the press, assembly, and the right to petition the government. And rightfully so. They were the architects behind the First Amendment. They made it happen. But Baptists held their feet to the fire to ensure the adoption of the First Amendment. Baptists' influence on those and other founders was unprecedented in this one critical area.

In fact, an impressive chorus of theologians, scholars, historians, and philosophers credit Baptists with this contribution to the new republic. One of those theologians, George W. Truett, delivered the greatest twentieth-century treatise on religious liberty. Truett, then pastor of First Baptist Church in Dallas, Texas, delivered an address May 16, 1920, on the east steps of the U.S. Capitol in conjunction with the annual meeting of the Southern Baptist Convention. Truett commented that religious liberty was America's chief contribution to civilization. "And historic justice compels me to say that it was preeminently a Baptist contribution," Truett said to the 10,000 to 15,000 people gathered there.

Truett backed his assertion with quotes from philosophers and historians. He pointed to John Locke's statement that "Baptists were the first propounders of absolute liberty, just and true liberty, equal and impartial liberty." Truett also noted a U.S. historian's assessment: "Freedom of conscience, unlimited freedom of mind, was from the first the trophy of the Baptists."

J. M. Dawson, the first executive director of the Baptist Joint Committee, wrote a significant work that traced the contributions of Baptists to the American republic:

> If the researchers of the world were to be asked who was most responsible for the American guaranty for religious liberty, their prompt reply would be "James Madison"; but if James Madison might answer, he would as quickly reply, "John Leland and the Baptists."[1]

Others have attested to Baptists' leadership in this area. William Lee Miller, professor of religious studies at the University of Virginia, tagged the Jeffersonians and the Baptists as the two chief movements that shaped church-state separation.[2] British theologian H. Wheeler Robinson said that to the Baptists belong "the distinction of being the first to claim and the first to apply fearlessly the unfettered principle of freedom for religion."[3] Former SBC President E. Y. Mullins said, "The sufficient statement of the historical significance of the Baptists is this: the competency of the soul in religion."[4]

Baptist historian H. Leon McBeth put it this way:

> In no other area has Baptists' witness proved clearer and more consistent than in their struggle for the right of persons to answer to God and not to government for religious beliefs and behavior.[5]

But why was this principle so important to Baptists? How did they come to expound separation of church and state, an arrangement that many thought would spell the demise of both? And most importantly, how did Baptists influence the founders to adopt that novel scheme as part of the Bill of Rights?

Baptists used the Scriptures, logic, and history to defend their radical view of religious freedom, according to McBeth.[6] Despite the fact that Baptists emerged in England at a time when government was hostile toward them, McBeth wrote, they drew their convictions directly from the Bible.

The Scriptures are replete with references regarding religious liberty. Religious freedom begins scripturally with the creation narratives. To be made in God's image is to be allowed choices guided by a free conscience (Gen 1–2). Throughout the history of Israel, the Scriptures reveal that freedom and liberty are keys to proper relationship to God.

In the New Testament, both Jesus and Paul discuss the liberty found in the person of Christ. Galatians 5:1 reads, "For freedom Christ has set us free. Stand firm, therefore, and do not submit to a yoke of slavery." As Jesus extended the invitation to "come follow me," his disciples and other believers came to him freely, or not really. Not in one single passage in the Old or New Testaments does coerced religion play a part in God's plan and purpose for creation.

The most commonly cited Scripture reference to church-state separation is Matthew 22:15-22. Indeed, Baptists contend that Jesus articulated the principle of separation when he said, "Give therefore to the emperor the things that are the emperor's, and to God the things that are God's." That simple admonition set forth the proper relationship between the two institutions. In his 1920 speech, Truett labeled Jesus' saying in Matthew 22 "one of the most revolutionary and history-making utterances that ever fell from those lips divine. That utterance, once for all, marked the divorcement of church and state." The New Testament places supreme emphasis on the individual, Truett added, noting that the doctrine of religious liberty came from the germinal concept of the lordship of Jesus Christ—the source of all Baptist doctrine.

But that deeply-held religious belief also had a practical application for Baptists. They needed the political protection of church-state separation to exercise their God-given religious freedom. A persecuted minority, they were beaten, jailed, horse-whipped, fined, harassed, maligned, taxed, ostracized, and ridiculed. Baptists' advocacy for religious freedom began before colonial times, harkening back to the intolerance of the Crown.

The seventeenth-century Baptist John Smyth proffered an early Baptist statement on religious liberty:

> That the magistrate is not by virtue of his office to meddle with religion, or matters of conscience, to force or compel men to this or that form of religion, or doctrine: but to leave Christian religion free, to every man's conscience, and to handle only civil transgressions.[7]

Other great Baptist champions of the conscience equated religious persecution with spiritual rape and denounced any earthly authority's meting out punishment in spiritual matters. A contemporary of Smyth, Thomas Helwys, wrote:

> Let them be heretickes, Turcks, Jewes, or whatsoever it apperteynes not the earthly power to punish them in the least measure (in spiritual matters).[8]

But perhaps no Baptist better propounded complete religious freedom than the founder of Rhode Island, Roger Williams. Williams, a Baptist for just a few months, founded the first Baptist church in America at Providence.

English settlers came to the New World largely to practice their religion without civil interference, but they brought their problems with them. In Maryland, Cecil Calvert extended a limited religious tolerance that excluded Jews, deists, and Unitarians, who could be executed for their beliefs. In Pennsylvania, the religious liberty door swung open, but not all the way. William Penn restricted those eligible for office to people who held a prescribed faith. Until the American Revolution, nine of the colonies supported an established church, leaving Rhode Island alone in granting complete religious liberty for all its citizens.[9]

Williams' radical state charter did not find immediate acceptance, however, and just how the colonies adopted his vision is not entirely clear, according to Baptist historian William R. Estep. We do know that other Baptists followed Williams, paving the way for the new nation to try his lively experiment. In fact, Estep says in his book, *Revolution within the Revolution*, that Williams' contribution had been all but forgotten when Isaac Backus began working with the Warren Baptist Association to ensure religious liberty. Backus wrote and traveled extensively to influence colonial thinking on religious freedom. Unfortunately, Backus' significant contributions often are overshadowed by John Leland, who is best remembered for his legendary meeting with James Madison. Baptists credit that encounter as a primary impetus to Madison penning the First Amendment.

The story goes like this: Leland decided to oppose Madison as a candidate to the Virginia convention that was called to ratify the new federal Constitution. Leland opposed his Virginia neighbor because Madison supported the original draft of the Constitution without an explicit guarantee for religious freedom. Madison seemed to believe that religious freedom had sufficient protection. Leland disagreed. After a private meeting between the two, Leland withdrew opposition, and Baptists supported Madison, who won. Later, Madison proposed a bill of rights. No one knows for sure what was said between the two men, but most assume they struck some sort of deal. Baptists point to this meeting as pivotal in the eventual ratification of the Bill of Rights in 1791, initiating a radical departure from previous forms of government.[10] That's the stuff folklore should be made of.

Notes

[1]Joseph Martin Dawson, *Baptists and the American Republic* (Nashville TN: Broadman, 1956) 117.

[2]William Lee Miller, *The First Liberty: Religion and the American Republic* (New York: Paragon House, 1988) 183.

[3]H. Wheeler Robinson, *The Life and Faith of the Baptists* (London: The Kingsgate Press, 1946) 123.

[4]"The Baptist Heritage Calendar," Baptist Joint Committee, Washington DC, 1992.

[5]Leon McBeth, *The Baptist Heritage: Four Centuries of Baptist Witness* (Nashville TN: Broadman, 1987) 252.

[6]Ibid., 86.

[7]John Smyth, quoted in William L. Lumpkin, ed., *Baptist Confessions of Faith* (Valley Forge PA: Judson Press, 1959, 1983) 140.

[8]Thomas Helwys, *The Mistery of Iniquity* (London, 1612) 69, quoted by McBeth, 86.

[9]Dawson, 2-3.

[10]Herschel Hobbs and E. Y. Mullins, *The Axioms of Religion* (Nashville TN: Broadman, 1978) 44-45.

Chapter 2

One Voice

"No man, no government nor institution, religious or civil, social or economic, has the right to dictate how a person may worship God, or whether he shall worship at all."

—The Baptist World Congress, 1939

What slavery tore apart in 1845, religious liberty began to restore in 1936—a united Baptist voice. For a brief period (1814–1845), Baptists in the United States were consolidated under one denominational umbrella. When the northern and southern regions of the country fought over slavery, Baptists followed suit, eventually splitting in 1845. But on May 16, 1936, Southern Baptists began a process that would reunite them for more than half a century. Baptists remained in their respective conventions but pooled their resources for one common principle: absolute religious freedom for all citizens. To that end, they planted the seeds for an agency whose sole purpose was to keep watch on the church-state intersection in the nation's capital. The Baptist Joint Committee became the first national organization that united Baptists across denominational lines in a joint endeavor.

The agency's current executive director, James M. Dunn, traces the BJC's roots to the 1936 meeting of the Southern Baptist Convention in St. Louis, Missouri. At that meeting, messengers voted to change the name and focus of an existing committee that was the precursor to the permanent office eventually established in Washington, D.C. The General Committee on Army and Navy Chaplains was renamed the Committee on Public Relations and given an additional mandate:

> As situations arise, in which agencies of this convention are compelled to confer, to negotiate, to demand just rights that are being threatened or to have other inescapable dealings with the American or other governments, this committee shall function, when so requested by any existing board or agency of this body, as the representative of Southern Baptists.

This 1936 entry into public affairs blossomed into a full-fledged office a decade later. The original members of the Committee on Public Relations were chair Rufus W. Weaver, D.C.; E. Hilton Jackson, D.C.; John Garland Pollard, D.C.; Perry

Mitchell, Virginia; and J. T. Watts, Maryland. In 1937, another distinguished Baptist, Senator Hugo Black of Alabama, was elected to represent the SBC on the committee. His tenure, however, was cut short when President Franklin D. Roosevelt nominated him to the U.S. Supreme Court, where he served for thirty-four years. Black and the agency crossed paths again as it filed friend-of-the-court briefs in controversial church-state cases he helped decide.

On May 25, 1937, the Northern Baptist Convention (NBC), now the American Baptist Churches in the USA, created a similar committee. Weaver, executive secretary of the District of Columbia Baptist Convention, was among the original NBC representatives; he is the only person who served simultaneously on both committees.

Southern Baptists may have been the first to enter the realm of public affairs, but Northern Baptists were the first to express a desire to work jointly:

> When principles held alike by Northern and Southern Baptists are in any way endangered, this committee shall be authorized to act in cooperation with the Committee on Public Relations, appointed by the Southern Baptist Convention.

Both committees began working together, and by 1939, they asked their respective denominations to allow them to operate formally as a joint committee. Northern Baptists quickly embraced the recommendation that would take Southern Baptists a few more years to approve. The National Baptist Convention, USA, the nation's largest African-American Baptist denomination, became involved in September 1939, initiating its own committee. That year also was pivotal because the three conventions, with a combined membership of 10.2 million, unanimously approved a pronouncement on religions liberty called "The American Baptist Bill of Rights" (see Appendix A).

In 1941, Southern Baptists transferred the military chaplaincy duties of its committee to the Home Mission Board and agreed to the principle of formally working with other denominations, while stopping short of a merger. Southern, Northern, and National Baptists worked for the cause of religious liberty through what became known as the Joint Conference Committee on Public Relations, which on September 1, 1946, resulted in a permanent office in Washington. During the formative decade, Weaver provided key leadership for the group that grappled with religious persecution in Rumania, the establishment of official U.S. relations with the Vatican, and the formation of the United Nations charter.

The group was tested early as it intervened on behalf of Baptist mission work in Rumania in 1937. The Rumanian Ministry of Cults and Arts issued a decree forbidding "religious proselytism," effectively cutting off Baptist mission work. The committee talked with State Department officials, one of whom was R. Walton Moore, whose great-grandfather Jeremiah Moore was imprisoned in Virginia for preaching the gospel.

This pressure resulted in only a temporary reopening of churches. By July 1938, Baptist activities again were restricted. The religious liberty committee's first meeting was held September 15-16, 1938, to address the Rumanian problem. The group drafted a position paper on the crisis and a petition to the Rumanian minister. The committee also published a pamphlet, written by Weaver, that prompted 2,000 telegrams to the minister protesting treatment of Baptists. The Baptist outcry was not heeded, however. Baptist churches were closed, and some preachers were imprisoned. Persistence finally brought victory, and Baptist churches were reopened. In 1940, the Rumanian government shocked Baptists by giving their churches an equal footing with other faith groups.

Many players helped lift this religious persecution. The Baptist World Alliance, founded in 1905 partly to help preserve religious liberty around the globe, deserved much credit, as did the new religious liberty group.

The most contentious issue during this early period was the establishment of formal diplomatic relations with the Vatican. The Joint Conference Committee fought that effort, and today, the BJC continues to oppose a U.S. ambassador to the Vatican as an affront to the Constitution.

In 1867, President Andrew Johnson ordered the American Ministry to the Vatican closed. According to a paper by Weaver, Johnson's actions were prompted by the fact that ambassadors to the Vatican were allowed to hold religious services in the embassies in 1866, but all other Protestant worship was forbidden in the city of Rome. But in 1939, President Roosevelt reopened the debate when he announced the appointment of Myron C. Taylor as personal envoy to the Vatican. The Joint Conference Committee protested in a letter:

> The distinctive theory, upon which this government has been founded, is the absolute separation of church and state, and any recognition, implied or otherwise, of the political status of any ecclesiastical organization constitutes, in our judgment, an assault upon this principle.

Roosevelt responded by inviting Weaver and a small delegation of religious leaders to the White House. Roosevelt told them during the thirty-minute meeting that he did not view the appointment as establishing formal diplomatic relations with the Vatican, but as an attempt to maintain world peace. Baptists countered that this represented a constitutional crisis of great importance. The appointment proceeded despite their sincere and staunch protests.

As World War II ended, the Joint Conference Committee wanted to ensure that religious liberty would not be the exclusive right of Americans. The group desired universal religious freedom for every global citizen. Weaver fervently advocated securing universal religious freedom as the only way to lasting peace, maintaining that such a cause was even more important than winning the war.

So, four Baptists—including J. M. Dawson, who later became the agency's first executive director—represented the Joint Conference Committee at the United Nations Conference in San Francisco in 1945. They presented the Baptist argument that universal religious liberty be incorporated into the U.N. charter. The Joint Conference Committee secured some 100,000 Baptist signatures supporting the inclusion of this principle. Although the U.N. charter did not contain a specific religious liberty provision, the effort contributed to the inclusion of the idea in principle in the preamble to the charter, according to Dawson in *A Thousand Months to Remember.*

During the first decade, the group also opposed aid to parochial schools, intervened on behalf of American and Southern Baptist missions work in China, and advocated humane treatment in the resettlement of Japanese Americans who had been detained following the 1941 attack on Pearl Harbor. Under Weaver's leadership, the Joint Conference Committee took flight, winning some battles and losing others, but always staying the course. Baptists, again, spoke as one.

Chapter 3

The Scorecard

"We believe that this contemplated permanent office in Washington is one of the most forward steps ever taken by American Baptists."
—C. E. Bryant
Editor, *Arkansas Baptist*

What do a statesman, a visionary, a scholar, and a fighter have in common? Answer: They all stood at the helm of the Baptist Joint Committee—sometimes in the form of four separate leaders, and other times as traits of the same man.

Joseph Martin Dawson, beloved pastor of First Baptist Church of Waco, Texas, helped get the agency moving as its first executive director. Perhaps no Baptist statesman in his time was better suited to help the new agency gain influence with legislators and among Baptists. C. Emanuel Carlson took the reins from Dawson, adding his unique vision to help the agency expand and grow. Academician James E. Wood Jr. continued the legacy by helping the BJC define itself and clarify its voice. And the inimitable James M. Dunn used his Texas tenacity to ward off those bent on destroying the agency in its David-and-Goliath confrontation with Southern Baptist fundamentalists.

Since the doors opened in 1946, these four men have made their mark on the agency, Baptist life, and the nation as a whole. The following is a cursory examination of their contributions.

The J. M. Dawson Years, 1946–1953

Dawson came to the BJC on August 1, 1946, with the understanding that he would retire when he turned seventy-five. Building on Weaver's work, Dawson established the organizational framework for the agency. Under his leadership, the agency secured office space, hired support staff, adopted a constitution, changed its name to the Baptist Joint Committee on Public Affairs, and initiated the publication of *Report from the Capital*. Dawson also fought hard to expand participation in the agency by other Baptist groups.

Among his greatest accomplishments was his role in the establishment of Protestants and Other Americans United (POAU) for the Separation of Church and State (now called Americans United for Separation of Church and State). While committed to the BJC, Dawson believed that the tiny agency's budget would not permit it to speak on behalf of the larger Protestant community. So, he sought another mechanism to accomplish that goal. He became POAU's first recording secretary when it was formally organized November 20, 1947, at Chicago's Methodist Temple. Dawson's passionate belief in universal religious liberty kept him from viewing the potentially rival organization as anything but an ally in the cause. Three executive directors later, that relationship remains intact.

Dawson's tenure made its greatest impact through the agency's involvement in public issues, including tax support for private and religious schools, religion and the public schools, diplomatic relations with the Vatican, government aid to sectarian hospitals, and global religious liberty.

Opposed to government funding of religious schools, the agency became involved in two significant Supreme Court cases under Dawson. The first case, *Everson v. Board of Education* (1947), involved a dispute over reimbursement for transportation costs to and from religious schools. BJC Chair E. Hilton Jackson, a constitutional lawyer, filed a brief opposing the practice in which a local school board reimbursed parents for sending their children to religious schools.

Despite the agency's efforts, a narrowly divided Supreme Court upheld the practice in a 5–4 decision. The court said that because the state paid the parents, not the schools, the New Jersey practice did not violate the establishment clause. Justice Hugo Black wrote the majority opinion:

> The First Amendment has erected a wall between church and state. That wall must be kept high and impregnable. We could not approve the slightest breach. New Jersey has not breached it here.

The agency disagreed with its former board member.

The agency's involvement in a second significant Supreme Court case embroiled it—for the first time—in a major Baptist controversy. In *McCollum v. Board of Education of Champaign (Ill.) County* (1948), the Supreme Court examined the constitutionality of "released time" religious instruction in the public school classrooms in Champaign, Illinois. Again, Jackson filed a BJC brief in opposition.

This position brought the agency into conflict with many Baptists. Unlike the *Everson* case, in which the agency had strong Baptist support, the BJC's position in *McCollum* proved to be its most controversial stance under Dawson. It seemed some Baptists opposed aid to parochial schools, but not religious instruction in public schools.

Among the most vocal critics was Duke K. McCall, executive secretary of the Southern Baptist Convention. McCall called the BJC brief "ill advised" and something that Southern Baptists could never support, according to an April 8, 1948, Associated Press article. McCall wanted the brief recalled, but the other supporting conventions wanted it kept in place; so it was.

This time the agency was pleased with the outcome: an 8–1 decision, again written by Black, that ruled such practice violated the establishment clause. The Court said:

> The operation of the state's compulsory education system thus assists and is integrated with the program of religious instruction carried on by separate religious sects. Pupils compelled by law to go to school for secular education are released in part from their legal duty upon the condition that they attend the religious classes. This is beyond all question a utilization of the tax-established and tax-supported public school system to aid religious groups to spread their faith. And it falls squarely under the ban of the First Amendment.

Dawson lauded the decision. McCall denounced it, causing tension between the agency and its largest member body. Dawson addressed the SBC Executive Committee to assuage its concerns. Jackson also worked to dispel misconceptions that *McCollum* was hostile toward religion. Dawson and Jackson succeeded as Southern Baptist Convention messengers voted in 1949 to support the decision.

The agency continued to fight against religious instruction in public schools. But the most time-consuming issue confronting Dawson was the appointment of a U.S. representative to the Vatican, an issue that has plagued every BJC executive director. President Harry S Truman had promised Baptist leaders that he would withdraw Myron S. Taylor from the Vatican after the signing of the peace treaties. When he reneged, the BJC launched a massive campaign for Taylor's recall. But the issue subsided temporarily when Taylor resigned in 1949.

Fearing Catholic officials would pressure the administration to appoint a replacement for Taylor, the BJC maintained a strong education campaign to oppose the notion. In January 1951, Religious News Service reported that Truman would not replace Taylor, but the apparent victory was short-lived. Ten months later he said he would appoint Mark W. Clark as ambassador to the Vatican. The Vatican apparently objected to a military man in the post, and Clark withdrew his nomination. In 1953, Truman left the White House to return to Missouri without nominating another person for the post.

Under Dawson's leadership, the agency also opposed channeling government funds to religious hospitals, compulsory military training in peacetime, and alcohol advertisements, and voiced concern about the status of "displaced persons" or immigrants. In addition, it endorsed a plan to admit 400,000 immigrants, and congressional action eventually opened U.S. borders to 200,000 of them.

The Dawson years laid the foundation for the ministry, which the board recognized in a resolution following his death on July 6, 1973:

> He achieved distinction among Baptists as pastor, author, and statesman, as chairman of the Southern Baptist Convention Executive Committee and publicity director of their $75 Million Campaign, and he was one of the first to raise his voice for equal rights for all peoples and worked untiringly for that goal.

The C. Emanuel Carlson Years, 1954–1971

A native of Alberta, Canada, Carlson succeeded Dawson in January 1954. The former dean of Bethel College, St. Paul, Minnesota, did not envision a long tenure for himself, but his seventeen-year stint still stands as the longest to date.

Carlson led the agency to examine its philosophy and organizational structure. He wanted the agency to adopt a proactive basis for its mission. Carlson strongly believed that the BJC ought to do more than react to threats to religious liberty as they arose. So, the agency studied the biblical basis for the relationship of church, state, and society, and implemented staff and structural changes accordingly.

Under Carlson's watch, the agency revised its constitution, added three full-time professional staff members, and expanded to nine the number of constituent bodies. The Progressive National Baptist Convention, an African-American convention, was the last to join, marking a milestone in the history of the agency that had struggled to attract African-American participation. Carlson credited the election of African-American Homer J. Tucker as chair (1969–1970) as pivotal in gaining full participation of African-American conventions.

In 1957, the BJC made its first professional staff addition. W. Barry Garrett, editor of the Arizona *Baptist Beacon,* was named associate director of information services. Within a few months, the SBC Executive Committee established a Washington Bureau of Baptist Press, and Garrett served as its editor. He received credentials from the House and Senate Press Galleries and the White House Press Corps. In the 1960s, he traveled to Rome as the only accredited Baptist reporter to the last three sessions of the Second Vatican Council. When Amy Carter, the daughter of President and Mrs. Jimmy Carter, was baptized, he went to the White House to help explain the Baptist view of baptism to reporters.

In 1965, Walfred H. Peterson joined the staff as director of research services. Peterson was a teacher at Bethel College and worked at the BJC for three years before leaving to accept a teaching post at Washington State University. He was succeeded by John W. Baker in 1969.

Prior to joining the BJC staff, Baker was chair of the political science department at the College of Wooster in Ohio. He also had an illustrious career with the BJC, serving as a driving force behind the enactment of the Equal Access Act of 1984. Baker, who earned a law degree while at the agency, became the BJC's first staff attorney. When Carlson retired, Baker also served as acting executive director for more than a year.

James M. Sapp became director of correlation services in 1964. Sapp helped develop relationships with state groups; became editor of *Report from the Capital,* freeing Garrett to focus on the news service; and planned the agency's religious liberty conferences.

The enhanced organizational structure was perhaps Carlson's greatest achievement. It better enabled the staff to work on public issues such as federal funding of private schools, religion in public schools, tax exemption for churches, federal aid to sectarian hospitals, diplomatic ties to the Vatican, and the 1960 election involving a Catholic presidential nominee.

Fighting federal aid to religious schools dominated the Carlson years. In particular, the agency voiced concerns over provisions in the Elementary and Secondary Education Act of 1965 that provided indirect benefits to parochial schools. Testifying before congressional committees, Carlson advocated that public funds should be used only for public purposes. The act opened the door to indirect aid to students at religious schools, but the question of direct aid had not been resolved.

The BJC and others maintained that government funding of religious institutions violated the establishment clause. In the face of staunch opposition, parochial aid advocates devised a system in 1970, whereby "vouchers" would be given to the parents to send their children to religious schools. Then, tax dollars would be paid to the schools in exchange for the voucher. The BJC reasoned that what could not go in the front door should not be allowed in the back door. Voucher advocates lost, and today this debate continues under the "parental choice" banner.

The agency also wrestled with several issues concerning the proper role of religion in the public square. The BJC successfully opposed a constitutional amendment declaring America a Christian nation, a measure to make Good Friday a legal holiday, and a proposed question on the 1960 census asking citizens to identify their religion.

During the Carlson years, the agency also responded to two of the most controversial Supreme Court decisions involving religion in the public schools. More than thirty years later, the nation continues to be divided by the 1962 and 1963 decisions on prayer and Bible reading in the public schools.

The first case, *Engel v. Vitale*, involved the daily recitation of a prayer sanctioned by the New York Board of Regents in the state's public school system. The prayer: "Almighty God, we acknowledge our dependence upon thee; and we beg thy blessings upon us, our parents, our teachers, and our country." In a 6–1 decision, the court barred prescribed prayer in public schools. The public outcry was perhaps the loudest and most sustained in American history. In *Report from the Capital*, Garrett likened the hew and cry to that experienced after the 1954 school desegregation decision. When the case was pending, the agency had not played an active role. But in the aftermath, it made a staunch defense of the decision:

> We think, along with the Court "that the constitutional prohi-
> bition against laws respecting an establishment of religion must
> at least mean that in this country it is no part of the business of
> government to compose official prayers for any group of the
> American people to recite as part of a religious program carried
> on by government."

The next year, the high court also ruled that it was unconstitu-
tional to require public school children to read the Bible and
recite the Lord's Prayer *(Abington v. Schempp and Murray v. Cur-
lett)*. These decisions did not cause a similar furor, but the entire
debate over religion in the public school continued to rage, leading to repeated attempts to rewrite the First Amendment. The BJC
opposed all attempts to alter America's first liberty, testifying in
Congress repeatedly against constitutional amendments designed
to tinker with the religion clauses.

The 1960 presidential race posed a unique problem. Many
feared that a Catholic president would submit his authority to the
Vatican. The BJC was among those concerned about Senator John
F. Kennedy's church-state views. On the other hand, the BJC
always had stood against religious bigotry and supported the
Constitution's prohibition against using religious tests as measures of a candidate's fitness for public office. So Carlson tried to
strike a balance between caution and overreaction.

On August 24, 1960, Carlson met with Kennedy for thirty
minutes. The two men emerged agreeing that "a frank renuncia-
tion by all churches of political power as a means to religious
ends would greatly improve the political climate and would seem
to be a legitimate request by both political parties," according to
a Baptist Public Affairs news story. Kennedy told Carlson he was
concerned because people opposed him based solely on his
church membership. Kennedy publicly announced his opposition to an ambassador to the Vatican and parochial aid, as well as
his support for church-state separation. After the election,
Kennedy's solid church-state record prompted the BJC board to
commend him in a formal resolution in 1961.

The Vatican issue continued to resurface during the Carlson
years, but not much transpired until 1970 when President
Richard Nixon appointed Henry Cabot Lodge as an "occasional
visitor" to the Vatican. The following year Carlson stepped down
from the BJC post, having helped the agency expand in size and
influence.

The James E. Wood, Jr. Years, 1972–1980

James E. Wood Jr. was a professor and director of the J. M. Dawson Institute for Church-State Studies at Baylor University in Waco, Texas, when he came to the BJC in 1972. Under Wood, the BJC worked on the same issues that confronted his two predecessors: U.S.-Vatican ties, government funding of religious schools, the role of religion in public schools, and universal religious freedom. But new issues emerged in the 1970s: expansion of Internal Revenue Service regulations related to churches, the use of missionaries for intelligence gathering, the nuclear arms race, the growth of the New Right, and abortion, to name a few.

Among the distinctions of the Wood years was the agency's foray into the abortion issue. Wood is the only BJC executive, in his official capacity, to go on record concerning abortion. His pro-choice position is part of the agency's October 2, 1973, minutes.

His predecessors had dabbled in issues outside the religious liberty arena such as alcohol and immigration, but under Wood's leadership the agency addressed a plethora of social issues. Prior to Wood's tenure, some criticized the agency for overstepping its mandate, but that criticism intensified under Wood. Eventually, confusion arose concerning which agency—the BJC or Southern Baptist Christian Life Commission—should grapple with social issues beyond the religious liberty field. Wood argued that God was sovereign over all of life, and to limit the BJC to religious liberty denied that fact. Further, he said that his views were consistent with the broad interests expressed by his predecessors. The agency's scope was to encompass all human rights, including religious liberty. (In fact, the BJC's work for equal justice for all people earned it the Isaiah Award from the American Jewish Committee in 1979, which marked the first time the award was given to an organization.)

Finally, the SBC intervened to clarify the two agencies' roles. In 1976, SBC messengers approved two motions indicating that the BJC was the sole office through which it would maintain contact with government officials and outlining the agency's duties. The CLC would attend to moral and social concerns; religious liberty and church-state separation would be left to the BJC. That would change nearly fifteen years later, when the revamped SBC would disown the BJC and give its religious liberty program assignment to the CLC.

Among the religious liberty issues Wood grappled with was the perennial diplomatic relations with the Vatican. Wood expressed personal disappointment when President Jimmy Carter, a Southern Baptist, appointed David M. Walters as an envoy to the Vatican on July 6, 1977.

Under Wood, the agency faced the usual religion in public school and parochial aid battles, but some new threats to religious liberty emerged. One occurred when the Equal Employment Opportunity Commission (EEOC) ruled that religious institutions could not consider religious beliefs in hiring employees. The EEOC maintained that to do so was a form of religious discrimination. The BJC countered that religious groups must be free to hire only those employees that have the same religious convictions.

In the 1970s, the Department of Labor tried to make Southern Baptists' largest seminary—Southwestern Baptist Theological Seminary in Fort Worth, Texas—comply with this regulation. Even though Southwestern was privately funded for a religious purpose, the government would not budge. Wood maintained that fundamental to American society was the right of religious organizations to preserve their religious character. Eventually the court concurred. In 1987, the Supreme Court ruled that religious institutions had the right to hire employees based on religious preferences *(Bishop v. Amos)*.

Also during Wood's tenure, the agency voiced grave concern about the danger of wedding the New Religious Right with the political right. The agency opposed then, and opposes today, the trend to use religion to support nationalism.

The agency also fought restrictive lobby disclosure bills that would have hampered the churches' prophetic witness, worked on tax issues involving churches, and was involved in foreign affairs. The committee, while disappointed that Carter appointed an envoy to the Vatican, went on record in 1977 to commend the president's emphasis on human rights in foreign policy.

The National Council of Churches also selected Wood as the only representative of U.S. churches to the Helsinki meetings, designed to implement the Helsinki Final Accords. The accords represent an international agreement on various human rights, including religious liberty.

Other international issues involved Baptist missionaries over-seas. U.S. citizens living in foreign countries were denied the right to vote. In 1973 testimony, the BJC asserted that this represented a violation of their rights. All Americans overseas were given vot-ing rights in 1976. Also, in 1976, Wood expressed concern over media reports that the Central Intelligence Agency (CIA) was using missionaries as spies. On occasion, missionaries were unaware that they were talking to CIA agents and had unwittingly been used for intelligence gathering. The BJC raised strong objec-tions to such practices.

The BJC also was involved in several court disputes involving aid to religious schools and opposed a new movement to provide tuition tax credits to parents so they could send their children to private, religious schools. Movements to reinstate state-sponsored school prayer also intensified. In 1971, a constitutional prayer amendment fell just twenty-eight votes shy in the House of Representatives.

In 1979, Senator Jesse Helms (R-NC) advocated removing the school prayer issue from the jurisdiction of the Supreme Court, a move opposed by the agency and President Carter but supported by SBC President Adrian Rogers. Wood criticized Rogers as con-tradicting Southern Baptist Convention resolutions supporting the 1960s public school prayer decisions. Rogers was the first in a long line of fundamentalists elected in the takeover of the SBC. This rift with Rogers was an early indication of a new day in Southern Baptist life and a new corresponding relationship with the religious liberty agency. Later, the skirmish over a constitu-tional amendment to reinstate state-sponsored school prayer in the 1980s would result in the SBC disowning the BJC.

After eight years, Wood returned to Baylor. His tenure at the helm of the BJC was by far the most diverse in dealing with public issues.

The James Dunn Years, 1981–Present

Longtime Southern Baptist leader Porter Routh provided interim leadership until the agency tapped James M. Dunn from the top post at the Texas Baptist Christian Life Commission (CLC). Immediately, Dunn made it clear that the BJC would deal only with religious liberty and church-state issues. He believed Southern Baptists had given abortion and other moral and social issues to the CLC.

This book's remaining chapters focus on the agency's struggles and accomplishments under Dunn and will not be presented in detail here. However, a few achievements deserve special emphasis.

Dunn enhanced the agency's reputation in international affairs. The Baptist Joint Committee:

• Continued to push for legislation to end the double taxation of missionaries who paid taxes in the United States and in their host countries, which became an increasing problem until 1980. With the help of Jim Wright in the House of Representatives and Mark Hatfield in the Senate, the Overseas Earned Income Act made it illegal to double-tax missionaries and other U.S. workers overseas. Keith Parks, former president of the Southern Baptist Foreign Mission Board, said this act saves Southern Baptists more than $1 million annually.

• Provided the U.S. State Department with a list of prisoners of conscience in the U.S.S.R. With delivery of the list to George Shultz, 116 prisoners of conscience, including Baptists, Muslims, and Jehovah Witnesses, were released.

• Worked closely with the Helsinki Commission and its chair, Representative Steny Hoyer (D-MD) on visas for persons in the former Union of Soviet Socialist Republics and Central Europe. (The Helsinki Commission, a shortened name for the Committee for Security and Cooperation in Europe, is an independent agency created by Congress to monitor compliance with human rights accords.)

• Helped represent evangelist Alex Awad in his effort to return to his native Israel and become the pastor of East Jerusalem Baptist Church.

• Worked with U.S. officials to clear the way for nearly fifty Baptist student missionaries to go to the former Soviet Union and remodel a church. They were the first such delegation allowed entry after the U.S.S.R. opened to religious groups.

Without question, Dunn's greatest feat was ensuring the agency maintained its integrity while under fire from the Southern Baptist Convention. Under duress, the agency never wavered from the bedrock Baptist principle that separation of church and state is the best way to safeguard religious liberty. Adherence to this principle, in the face of intense pressure, was even more significant than the agency's survival. For what good would it have done the BJC to survive without its essential core?

*Joseph Martin Dawson, first
executive director, 1946–1953.*

*C. Emanuel Carlson shares a laugh with Vice
President Hubert H. Humphrey at 1967 Religious
Liberty Conference, "The Role of the Christian
Through Church and State in Human Welfare."*

*James E. Wood Jr. (left) and Memphis pastor
Adrian Rogers discuss prayer in public schools at
SBC Executive Committee meeting, Feb. 1980.*

Chapter 4
To Pray or Not to Pray?

"But for the Baptist Joint Committee, there would not be an Equal Access Act."

—Barry Lynn
Americans United for Separation of Church and State

While the Baptist Joint Committee held open the door, the nation's high court and atheist Madalyn Murray O'Hair kicked God out of public school. Right?

Such absurd rhetoric has characterized the national debate about the proper role of religion in public school since the 1962 Supreme Court decision striking down state-sponsored prayer. That ruling blew the lid off the Court, eliciting the strongest public outrage since the 1954 school desegregation decision, wrote W. Barry Garrett in *Report from the Capital.*

The school prayer decision still divides much of America. The reason? The inherent tension between the First Amendment's religion clauses. Both are designed to protect religious practice, but in different ways. Though both require governmental neutrality toward religion, they often rub against each other, at least in the short run.

For decades, opponents of the school prayer decision sought in vain for a remedy. Many of them believed that God had been exiled from the classroom and that, as a result, the morality of America's youth was declining. On the other hand, groups such as the BJC believed that the omnipotent God still had a perfect attendance record in public school and that the nation's ills stemmed from more complex problems.

The battle raged for decades, becoming part of presidential politics in the 1980s. President Ronald Reagan touted a constitutional amendment to reinstate government-sponsored school prayer, while both sides dug in their foxholes to engage the enemy. Although neither side would budge, each had the same goal: protection for religious rights of students in public schools. This revelation, along with the desire of some to find common ground, eventually led to the enactment of the Equal Access Act in 1984 (see Appendix B). But the road to enactment was treacherous, with the BJC bridging the ravine.

The BJC became involved in the equal access battle for three reasons. First, it was the right thing to do. Second, the religious liberty agency was at odds with one of its parent denominations. The Southern Baptist Convention went on record in 1982 supporting the Reagan prayer amendment, while the BJC opposed it. Third, in the context of this national debate, the agency looked for something proactive it could do to further free exercise rights. The staff and its board had tired of merely standing against something, even though they never wavered from their opposition to rewriting the Constitution.

In the battle for enactment, the religious liberty agency found itself engaged against some opponents who typically were allies. Among the most crucial were the Americans Civil Liberties Union (ACLU) and Representative Don Edwards (D-CA), who chaired the House Judiciary Committee. The BJC, the ACLU, and Representative Edwards usually would come down on the same side of the establishment clause—but not this time, according to Gary McNeil, who worked closely with the BJC's John Baker and Rosemary Brevard in this legislative battle.

Fortunately for the BJC and the equal access bill, one longtime BJC friend in the U.S. Senate saw the value in the legislation. On March 15, 1983, Senator Mark Hatfield (R-OR) introduced the bill "to provide that it shall be unlawful to discriminate against any meetings of students in public secondary schools" (S. 815). The premise: If students could meet before and after school for the chess club, then they could meet for Bible clubs. Hatfield said:

> Unfortunately, a growing number of federal court decisions have singled out religious speech as violative of the First Amendment to the U.S. Constitution when it involves only student-initiated groups that seek equal access to the use of school premises during nonclassroom hours. The bill I am reintroducing would provide a judicial remedy for high school students who are aggrieved by a discriminatory policy that is formulated and carried out by public schools which receive federal financial assistance.
>
> The bill is a straightforward measure to apply the Supreme Court's decision in *Widmar v. Vincent* to public high schools which receive federal aid. In *Widmar*, the court held that, absent a compelling purpose, a public university may not deny the use of it facilities to student groups who wish to meet and speak on religious subjects if it makes its facilities generally available to student groups for meetings on nonreligious subjects.

The court based this holding not on the free exercise of religion clause, but on the freedom of speech clause of the First Amendment.

The debate became murky when Senator Jeremiah Denton (R-AL) introduced other equal access legislation. Hatfield's bill was limited to secondary students and required that the meetings be student-initiated and student-controlled. Denton's bill would have included elementary schools.

In June 1983, the Senate Judiciary Committee held a hearing on the bills, with fifteen witnesses favoring equal access and only one group—the ACLU—opposing it. Speaking for the Reagan administration, Education Secretary Terrel H. Bell said the measure would "merely put voluntary religious activities on an equal footing with other extracurricular activities."[1]

It is important to note that although the BJC and Reagan administration clashed over the constitutional amendment to restore state-sponsored prayer, tuition tax credits, the Vatican ambassador, and more, they were united in the equal access effort. (Reagan resisted equal access in the beginning but supported it once his constitutional amendment failed.) In fact, the BJC's position drew fire from some its traditional supporters who said the agency was catering to SBC fundamentalists because of their attacks. And some fundamentalists, on the other side, criticized equal access as an inadequate substitute for the Reagan prayer amendment.

But the BJC persevered. In an October 25, 1983, statement to a House subcommittee, the BJC reiterated its case. The BJC had filed a brief with the Supreme Court in *Widmar* asserting that a student-initiated religious group had a constitutional right to meet on a university campus that had established a limited public forum. The same should hold true for secondary students, the BJC argued. But the agency would draw the line at including elementary school students because they do not engage in

> voluntary extracurricular activities—at the most they choose between activities offered by someone else. The lack of maturity in elementary school pupils requires that their school day be rigidly structured and supervised.
>
> The introduction of religion at this level would be neither voluntary nor student initiated.

The main BJC concerns included the following: Meetings must be completely voluntary and student-initiated; government or its agents, such as teachers or school boards, may not sponsor the meeting of any religious group; public funds beyond the expense of furnishing the facilities must not be spent for any religious meeting.

Hatfield's measure fit the bill. Representative Don Bonker (D-WA) sponsored the House companion (H.R. 4172) to Hatfield's bill. He told the subcommittee that he strongly supported the concept of equal access:

> When a school opens its facilities to student groups during noninstructional periods, it should not be allowed to discriminate against students who wish to meet voluntarily for religious purposes. . . . It is clearly inequitable to prevent students at public secondary schools from meeting voluntarily for religious purposes during noninstructional periods when the school permits student meetings for virtually any other legitimate purpose.
>
> Such a double standard is inconsistent with the principles of free speech and government neutrality toward religion.

The agency and other groups, such as the National Council of Churches, Seventh-day Adventists, the National Association of Evangelicals, and the Christian Legal Society, continued to push equal access. At its March 1984 meeting, the BJC board adopted a statement of support for the equal access bill, saying,

> When a public school establishes a limited public forum consisting of meetings of non-school-sponsored, student-initiated, and student-controlled, exclusively student groups, no group may be excluded on the basis of the religious content of the speech used in its meetings. . . . Any so-called "equal access" bill which meets these criteria should be actively promoted by the staff of this committee.

Pointing to this statement, BJC Executive Director James M. Dunn testified before a House subcommittee later that month, according to a Baptist Press article. He told the panel that the Hatfield-Bonker bill would help school officials "in making difficult decisions about the proper role of religion in the public school classroom" and would reduce the pressure on Congress to pass a school prayer amendment.

Religious News Service also reported the rift between traditional allies at the hearing. The National Council of Churches supported equal access while "its Jewish and civil liberties allies" stood against it, according to RNS. Much of the opposition stemmed from concerns that those who support school prayer would try to expand equal access to achieve their aim, using the new law to proselytize other students.

Also testifying before the House panel, Senator Hatfield told lawmakers that equal access was not "a backdoor approach to get government and school officials into the business of sponsoring, promoting, and influencing religious activities," according to Baptist Press. At the same hearing, Representative Edwards spoke against the measure.

In April 1984, the House Education and Labor Committee approved, 30–3, the bill for consideration on the House floor. The House considered the bill under suspension of rules—a legislative tactic that limits debate, bars amendments, and requires a two-thirds favorable vote, rather than a majority, for passage. Representatives Carl Perkins and William Goodling shaped that lopsided committee vote, McNeil said.

Chair of the House Education and Labor Committee Carl Perkins (D-KY) said the House needed to consider the measure under suspension of rules because of "time pressures" with the congressional calendar, which is typically shorter in an election year. But the equal access supporters fell eleven votes shy, with a 270–151 vote.

The overwhelming committee support indicated "smooth sailing" until "the opposition began an all-out campaign to derail" the bill, wrote the Christian Legal Society's Samuel Ericsson in a May 16, 1984, memo to CLS members and friends. He continued:

> Led by the ACLU and the National Educational Association, hundreds of lobbyists descended on Congress. They announced that equal access was the "son of school prayer," "school prayer through the backdoor," "devious," and would "subvert the First Amendment" and "undermine American democracy."
>
> The media joined in. *The Washington Post* ran an unprecedented four editorials filled with misinformation, half-truths, and outright falsehoods.

But the battle was far from over. A victory in the U.S. Senate could resuscitate the measure, but the ACLU was a formidable obstacle. One night, McNeil met the ACLU's Barry Lynn by coincidence at a concert. He asked Lynn, "We're not that far apart are we?" Lynn responded, "No." So, McNeil arranged for Lynn to meet with the BJC's Baker to discuss possible compromise language. Bolstered by the narrow defeat in the House, Baker worked with Lynn to draft language, expanding the bill's free speech application to include "religious, political, philosophical, or other" forms of speech. With the new language, the ACLU dropped its opposition.

Key lawmakers embraced the compromise. Senators Hatfield and Denton also reached a compromise, limiting coverage to secondary schools. An amended equal access provision was attached to a math-science bill, and on June 27, 1984, the Senate approved it on an 88–11 vote.

Even though equal access had broad support within the religious community, Senate supporters pointed to the BJC's leadership as crucial. Hatfield's press secretary, Rick Rolf, told Baptist Press:

> The senator is very appreciative of the work done by a number of groups who really exemplified the highest form of constructive channeling of passions over this issue. And clearly one of these groups at the forefront of all these negotiations that helped to get us there was the Baptist Joint Committee.

But the Senate-approved bill hit an immediate barrier when House Speaker Thomas P. O'Neill Jr. (D-MA) opposed it. The math-science bill had been approved by the House, but not with the equal access amendment. Representative Perkins wanted the bill to go to conference, but O'Neill thwarted him, according to an Associated Press article in the June 29, 1984, *Washington Post*. O'Neill referred the measure to two committees, one chaired by Perkins and the other by equal access opponent Representative Edwards. So, Perkins threatened to bring the bill to the floor through an unusual tactic, known as "Calendar Wednesday." The rules authorize committee chairs to bring bills to the floor on Wednesdays for a two-hour debate and a subsequent vote.

Equal access opponents did not want Perkins to use Calendar Wednesday, because they thought it might encourage other committee chairs to follow suit with other controversial provisions.

They also realized that Perkins had a compromise bill supported by an overwhelming majority of the Senate. On July 25, 1984, the House overwhelmingly approved, 337–77, the measure. And on August 11, 1984, President Reagan signed the bill into law.

Equal access supporters were elated that the long battle had been won, but their celebration was muted when Representative Perkins died eight days after the House approved the bill. The cover of the September 1984 issue of *REPORT from the Capital* honored contributions of the former chair of the House Education and Labor Committee:

> We came to admire, respect, and rely on the strength, skill, and savvy of this Baptist Congressman from eastern Kentucky. The fight for equal access underscored the chairman's commitment to moral legislation. There was no stopping his dogged persistence. He was always saying, "You Baptists must stay here all night talking to congressmen and letting your people know to call their representatives." Along with the attributes of moral concern, persistence, and compromise, Mr. Perkins added humility to his achievements. After final passage of equal access, Mr. Perkins did not attend any press conference. "The chairman does not go for this media recognition: the record will show who did what, and he will get his due," a staff member explained. Indeed the record shows that Carl Perkins was a champion. He fought the good fight, finished the course, and kept the faith.

John Baker in his monthly column in *Report* wrote that if any one person should be most-credited with the bill's passage that person would have to be Perkins. But there was plenty of credit to be shared, according to McNeil. In addition to Perkins, McNeil credits the BJC and the leadership of the late John Baker:

> Without Baker's credibility on church-state positions, there would have been no equal access act. Representative Don Edwards knew Baker and the BJC had been consistent on its church-state work and could not be linked to the conservative agenda.
>
> Being against the school prayer amendment, tuition tax credits gave the BJC a unique position to lead this work. One liberal member of the Education and Labor Committee started a meeting with Baker and myself saying, "I would not meet with you if you did not have such a solid reputation on church-state issues."

Baker carried the legislation by organizing the vote count, building the coalition, and "keeping the door open to the opponents," McNeil said.

Other individuals singled out by McNeil included Senator Hatfield, whose leadership drove the bill; Representative William Goodling (R-PA), the Republican leader on the Education and Labor Committee; Representative Don Bonker (D-WA), who stayed "on the front line" despite heat from his party; Representative Mike Synar (D-OK), who supported the compromise Senate bill; Phil Strickland of the Texas Christian Life Commission, who provided strategic assistance in vote counting; Sam Ericsson and the Christian Legal Society; Gary Ross and the Seventh-Day Adventists; Forest Montgomery and the National Association of Evangelicals; and Rosemary Brevard, the longest tenured assistant to the general counsel, serving more than twenty-five years before retiring in 1993.

Other observers lauded the BJC. Missouri Baptist editor Bob Terry wrote an editorial in the August 2, 1984, *Word & Way*, declaring the bill "a victory for the Baptist Joint Committee":

> Southern Baptists owe James Dunn and the staff of the Baptist Joint Committee on Public Affairs (BJCPA) sincerest congratulations and heartfelt gratitude for their role in the battle for prayer and Bible study in public schools. While other players have grabbed more headlines than the Baptist Joint Committee, it should not be forgotten that equal access legislation had its birth in the Joint Committee.

In March 1981, the BJC board instructed the staff to seek a way to ensure the rights of secondary school students to meet for prayer, Bible study, and other religious purposes, Terry recounted.

> By early spring of 1982, BJCPA staff members were meeting with sympathetic lawmakers, both Republicans and Democrats, in both houses of Congress. The going was not easy. President Reagan opposed the equal access concept, preferring instead his own prayer amendment. Several prominent TV evangelists opposed equal access. Even Southern Baptists were so busy debating the prayer amendment that securing support for equal access legislation was difficult. But the BJCPA staff was persistent.

When the prayer amendment was defeated, President Reagan and other earlier opponents threw their support behind equal access, Terry added:

> Members of Congress know the important role the BJCPA played in the struggle for religious liberty through adoption of equal access legislation. Members of Congress know the expertise and hard work of the BJCPA staff members.
>
> Southern Baptists should also recognize these qualities of the Baptist Joint Committee staff and express appreciation to James Dunn and others for their leadership.

Note

[1]*Report from the Capital,* Baptist Joint Committee (June 1983) 9.

James M. Dunn talks with U.S. Supreme Court Justice Harry A. Blackmun during a March 1990 briefing for Baptist editors sponsored by the BJC.

James M. Dunn talks with Warren E. Burger, retired chief justice of the U.S. Supreme Court, during the March 1993 conference sponsored by the Freedom Forum First Amendment Center.

Chapter 5
Liberty versus Luxury

"The Religious Freedom Restoration Act is the most important religious liberty bill in our lifetimes."

—Rabbi David Saperstein
Religious Action Center of Reform Judaism

L uxury, as defined by Webster, means a nonessential item or service that contributes to indulgence. But Supreme Court Justice Antonin Scalia must not have consulted his pocket dictionary on April 17, 1990. On that date, he tagged long-held legal protections for religious liberty as a "luxury" this nation could no longer afford. With the stroke of his pen, Scalia dropped a constitutional bombshell that shocked the religious community and gutted the free exercise clause of the First Amendment. America's first liberty was all but dead.

Scalia wrote the devastating opinion in *Employment Division v. Smith*, a case that church-state specialists say should have been routine—a "yawner." Alfred L. Smith and Galen W. Black were fired from a drug rehabilitation organization for using the illegal drug peyote in a worship ceremony of the Native American Church. The men were denied unemployment benefits because they had been fired for misconduct. But the Native Americans believe that peyote turns into the flesh of God when ingested, so they countered that they had a constitutional right to the sacramental use of peyote. The Oregon courts agreed, ruling that state laws prohibited the use of peyote, but that the free exercise clause protected its sacramental use. The state courts ruled that the federal constitutional protection outweighed the Oregon law. So, the question before the U.S. Supreme Court: Does the government have a compelling interest in denying this religious practice?

Court watchers were divided on how justices would decide the case. Some observers thought justices would rule in favor of the Native Americans, because several states and the federal government exempt the sacramental use of peyote from criminal prosecution. Others thought the court might rule against them, because the state had a compelling interest in stamping out illegal drug use that could trump free exercise claims. For three decades, the court had used the "compelling interest test" to decide these cases. The test stipulates that government must have an "interest of the highest order," such as health or safety, before it can impede the religious practices of its citizens. Experts debated whether the sacramental use of peyote would be protected by this high standard. But practically no one predicted that the court would jettison the protective standard, leaving everyone's religious exercise vulnerable to the whims of Caesar.

In reversing the Oregon court, the Supreme Court did just that. The high court virtually abandoned the compelling interest test for religious practice. Under *Smith*, government must simply demonstrate a rational basis, rather than a compelling interest, for its action. This ruling relegated religious freedom to the back of the bus as the only First Amendment right not to receive this high level of protection. Only when a free exercise claim could be coupled with another constitutional right, or when religion is targeted for discrimination, would it receive this shield.

In writing the opinion, Justice Scalia said that applying the compelling interest test to free exercise claims in an increasingly pluralistic society is a luxury the nation can no longer afford. He admitted that

> leaving accommodation to the political process will place at a relative disadvantage those religious practices that are not widely engaged in; but that unavoidable consequence of democratic government must be preferred to a system in which each conscience is a law unto itself.

How could a justice spout such majoritarian rhetoric? Trampling on minority religious practices is not the inevitable result of a democratic society—at least not in a country that for more than 200 years has explicitly protected those minority rights in the First Amendment.

Justice Sandra Day O'Connor took exception to Scalia's opinion. She agreed with the outcome—that the unemployment benefits should be denied—but did not want to abandon the compelling interest test. She called the opinion a dramatic departure from "well-settled First Amendment jurisprudence" that "is incompatible with our nation's fundamental commitment to individual religious liberty."

O'Connor quoted Justice Robert Jackson in *West Virginia Board of Education v. Barnette:*

The very purpose of a Bill of Rights was to withdraw certain subjects from the vicissitudes of political controversy, to place them beyond the reach of majorities and officials and to establish them as legal principles to be applied by the courts. One's right to life, liberty, and property, to free speech, a free press, freedom of worship and assembly, and other fundamental rights may not be submitted to vote; they depend on the outcome of no elections.

But while the high court was deeply and narrowly divided over the *Smith* decision, the religious community was not. Virtually every religious group was opposed to the rule in *Smith*, and the three-year battle to reverse its draconian effects was engaged.

Just days after the court handed down Smith, attorneys for twenty religious and civil liberties groups and fifty-five law professors petitioned the court for a rehearing. The petition read:

Every religious group in the country will be profoundly disadvantaged by the majority's rule. Under it, government could, for example, without constitutional impediment, bar all "non-humane" slaughter, and thus effectively outlaw Jewish and Moslem ritual slaughter; outlaw as medically unnecessary all circumcision, including that practiced for religious reasons by Jews, Moslems, and Coptic Christians; and outlaw all use of alcoholic beverages, including that used for communion and other religious purposes by Catholics and other Christians.

The petition continued that Jewish children in public school could be forced, under a no-hat rule, to remove their yarmulkes.

Those concerns were well-grounded. Just two days after the *Smith* decision, the high court cited it as the rationale for vacating an order concerning the rights of Amish claimants in Minnesota. In that case, the state wanted the Amish to place orange reflective signs on their buggies. Because of their religious convictions, the Amish did not want such garish signs on their buggies. The Minnesota Supreme Court approved a compromise, ruling that the Amish could use silver reflective tape that was less ostentatious. After the *Smith* decision, the Minnesota high court again ruled in favor of the Amish on state constitutional grounds. The state constitution now afforded Minnesotans more religious freedom than the Bill of Rights.

In the petition for rehearing, the coalition also criticized the court's decision for its unabashed judicial activism in reaching beyond the issue briefed and argued in the case. "Despite its protestations to the contrary, the Court has taken a major step away from settled law," the petition stated.

The court denied the rehearing. So the coalition, now called the Coalition for the Free Exercise of Religion, mounted a legislative campaign. On July 26, 1990, the Religious Freedom Restoration Act (RFRA) was introduced in the U.S. House of Representatives. The bill, sponsored by Representative Stephen Solarz (D-NY), would not mandate the outcome of a particular court case but would restore the standard by which it would be decided. In other words, it gave religious claimants a fighting chance, but not a sure victory.

On October 26, Senator Joseph Biden (D-DE) introduced a companion bill. But RFRA died in committee when the 101st Congress adjourned two days later. Working to revive the measure in the 102nd Congress, the coalition asked the BJC to serve as its chair largely because the BJC did not deal with abortion, occupied a centrist position in the diverse group, and was "represented by the charismatic Buzz Thomas," according to BJC Executive Director James M. Dunn. On June 26, 1991, Representative Solarz reintroduced RFRA, but it sat idle in Congress for more than a year without any Senate action. A bipartisan initiative to restore America's first freedom to its rightful place would have to wait while abortion politics ensnared it.

Several groups opposed or withdrew support for RFRA based on their fears that it would give a new constitutional right to abortion in the event *Roe v. Wade* was overturned. Reagan-Bush appointments gave anti-abortion advocates a majority on the high bench, and they anticipated the high court would overturn *Roe* at the first opportunity. Among the anti-abortion RFRA opponents were the National Right to Life Committee and the U.S. Catholic Conference. Although the U.S. Catholic Conference virtually was alone in the religious community, its political clout was formidable.

Mark Chopko, general counsel of the U.S. Catholic Conference, assured the coalition that the bishops opposed *Smith*, but they had three concerns. The bishops wanted three exemptions so that people could not use RFRA to challenge: the tax-exempt status of churches, the use of government funds for religious purposes, and any restriction on abortion.

The coalition had anti-abortion and pro-choice members who were divided over this issue, but they rallied behind the principle of religious freedom. So, the coalition steadfastly opposed any attempt to add exemptions to the bill.

BJC general counsel Oliver S. Thomas, who helped write RFRA and chaired the coalition, wrote:

> The beauty of RFRA is its adherence to a principle —religious liberty for all Americans. Activists from Paul Weyrich to Nadine Strossen have been willing to lay aside their deep ideological differences to restore the nation's first liberty to its rightful preeminence.

In an article for *The Florida Bar Journal*, J. Brent Walker, BJC associate general counsel, wrote:

> These exemptions are unfair, perhaps unconstitutional, unnecessary, and certainly impolitic. First, they are unfair and belie the across-the-board restoration principle upon which the RFRA coalition was originally based and the bill was introduced. The idea was and always has been to restore everyone's right to heightened protection without endorsing or excluding any particular claim.

The National Association of Evangelicals (NAE) was among the anti-abortion groups backing the bill. Robert Dugan Jr., director of the NAE Office of Public Affairs, called the bill "abortion neutral" at a press conference when it was reintroduced in the House of Representatives. Dugan said,

> We think the argument that the Supreme Court might overturn *Roe v. Wade* and then discover a right to abortion under a different label is little short of frivolous. RFRA simply restores a legal standard; it confers no new substantive rights, whether to abortion or any other claim based on free exercise of religion.

But abortion politics kept the Southern Baptist Christian Life Commission (CLC) at the periphery. CLC General Counsel Michael Whitehead conveyed the agency's concerns in a May 15, 1991, letter to Texas law professor Douglas Laycock. Whitehead said the CLC wanted to remedy *Smith* but could only support RFRA "if there is some way to guarantee our people (at least through the promises of a pro-life legal scholar) that not one baby will die under a colorable claim of RFRA protection." Laycock responded in a letter to Whitehead that his "worst fears are unfounded." RFRA would not result in the death of the unborn, he said.

Eventually, the CLC joined the coalition, which also included groups ranging from the American Civil Liberties Union and People for the American Way to Concerned Women for America and the Traditional Values Coalition. One group conspicuously absent from the RFRA debate was Pat Robertson's Christian Coalition; its silence on RFRA shouted volumes to the religious community. The Christian Coalition, which makes noise about an anti-Christian bias in society, could not be bothered to thwart a real threat. Perhaps restoring a legal test to heighten religious protection was not sexy enough to capture the right headlines or was not the most viable political tool for the Christian Coalition.

Abortion politics continued to plague RFRA. On November 26, 1991, Representatives Christopher Smith (R-NJ) and Henry Hyde (R-IL) introduced a separate bill (H.R. 4040). Supporters said it would rectify *Smith* without emboldening abortion rights. The coalition opposed any bill that was not abortion neutral.

Thirteen months after RFRA's reintroduction in the House, a companion bill was reintroduced in the upper chamber by Senators Orrin Hatch (R-UT) and Edward Kennedy (D-MA). According to procedure, RFRA was referred to committees in both chambers. Thomas joined a distinguished panel of witnesses testifying before the Senate Judiciary Committee on September 18, 1992. He told senators,

> Since *Smith* was decided, governments throughout the U.S. have run roughshod over religious conviction. Churches have been zoned out of even commercial areas. Jews have been subjected to autopsies in violation of their families' religious faith. A Catholic shelter for the homeless was closed because it could not afford an elevator, even though the nuns said they would carry any disabled up the stairs. In time, every religion in America will suffer.

Thomas said the bill would not create a new statutory right to abortion, jeopardize the tax-exempt status of churches, or hinder government partnerships with religious organizations to provide social services. Thomas, a member of the Supreme Court and an ordained minister, continued,

> Leading pro-life scholars and most pro-life organizations now agree that RFRA is scrupulously neutral on abortion and will not jeopardize the interests of pro-life groups. The Senate need not take my word for it. Your own nonpartisan Congressional Research Service has confirmed RFRA's abortion neutrality.

Thomas pointed to the pro-life groups in the sixty-eight-member coalition: the Christian Legal Society, Coalitions for America, NAE, CLC, Traditional Values Coalition, and more. "We implore you not to allow a relatively small group of pro-life advocates to hold religious liberty hostage until RFRA is rendered 'politically correct.' "

Chopko rebutted Thomas's testimony. He told senators that the U.S. Catholic Conference

> has legitimate concerns that S. 2969 will be utilized to attempt to promote the destruction of innocent unborn human lives, and to pit religious groups and individuals against one another in disputes over a variety of social and education programs as well as tax-exempt status. These concerns are based on years of experience in the public arena.

James Bopp Jr., general counsel of the National Right to Life Committee, also opposed RFRA without an abortion exemption. Bopp told the panel,

> The abortion-on-demand movement is urgently seeking new moorings for a constitutional right to abortion because of the ongoing scholarly and judicial rejection of the *Roe v. Wade* abortion privacy analysis. Pro-abortion partisans have repeatedly and forcefully asserted a free-exercise-of-religion right to abortion.

But Forest Montgomery, counsel for the NAE Office of Public Affairs, said the abortion argument was "farfetched" before the Supreme Court's 1992 decision in *Planned Parenthood v. Casey,* but "after *Casey* it is untenable." Court observers thought the high court might use *Casey* to overturn the 1973 decision that recognized a woman's right to privacy in abortion decisions. Instead, the court reaffirmed the essential holding in *Roe.* Montgomery,

whose organization never wavered from its support of RFRA or its
opposition to abortion, said:

> Thus there is no need to assert a religiously based right to abor-
> tion. When it comes down to obeying God or Caesar, the
> devout have no choice. Which is to say that *Employment Division
> v. Smith*—unless rectified—will inevitably lead to civil dis-
> obedience.
>
>   While we concede that free exercise is not an absolute, and
> that it must yield to compelling governmental interest, we can-
> not but remonstrate against the present rule which requires
> virtually no justification whatsoever for the abridgement of
> religious freedom.

But religious freedom advocates lost in 1992. Even though
the House Judiciary Committee approved RFRA, Congress
adjourned before the House voted on it. The bill died in the
Senate Judiciary Committee after Senator Alan Simpson (R-WY)
put a hold on the measure four days before Congress adjourned.

Simpson said in an October 2 statement that he did not want
the Senate to "rush through something as important as this." He
said he had unresolved questions about Congress's authority to
legislate such constitutional provisions:

> I am not yet comfortable that we know the answers to these and
> other questions. I would like to take more time to be certain
> that we are accomplishing exactly what we intend, and for these
> reasons, I ask that the bill be held over until our next meeting.

The stall, however, met with substantial criticism. Charles
Levendosky of the *Casper Star-Tribune* in Wyoming wrote a column, saying that religious liberty is being held "hostage to
anti-abortion forces." Other observers speculated whether the
abortion politics surrounding RFRA also had an impact on how
the presidential candidates responded to the measure during the
1992 election. President George Bush, an anti-abortion advocate,
was conspicuously silent on RFRA; he never tried to use the bully
pulpit of the White House to convince Congress to move the bill.
On the other hand, pro-choice Democratic nominee Bill Clinton
repeatedly voiced support for the bill while campaigning.

The NAE's Montgomery told a group of Baptist editors on
October 4, 1992, that the Bush administration did not help
because he suspected the White House did not want to get
involved during an election year. "The White House cares so

much for religious freedom it hasn't raised a finger," Montgomery added.

In an October 7 letter to the coalition, Thomas attributed the second death of RFRA to several factors, the most devastating of which was aggressive opposition by the Catholic Conference. Coalition members knew they had to get the Catholic Conference on board in the next session of Congress. To that end, negotiations with Catholic Conference officials continued with renewed intensity. The Catholic Conference finally endorsed RFRA after a meeting in the BJC conference room. The coalition struck a deal with the Catholics that satisfied them while securing the integrity of the bill.

According to the agreement, report and statutory language was added to clarify that the bill was not designed to create a new statutory right to abortion or to affect the tax-exempt status of churches or government funding of social programs. The BJC's Walker said the agreement did not alter the bill, but rather language was added to address more explicitly what the drafters intended in the first place. The legal effect of RFRA would be unchanged, Walker said. Thomas described the new language as a "clarification."

On March 9, 1993, the Catholic Conference officially endorsed RFRA. Two days later it was reintroduced in Congress, and President Clinton endorsed it that same day. The congressional sponsors of the new bill included Senators Kennedy and Hatch, and Representatives Charles Schumer (D-NY) and Christopher Cox (R-CA).

On March 17, 1993, a House subcommittee approved RFRA (H.R. 1308) for consideration by the House Judiciary Committee, which took just five days to clear RFRA for floor action. On May 11, the House unanimously approved RFRA on voice vote—a significant accomplishment, according to the BJC's Dunn.

"As a veteran Washington lobbyist, I've seen few such resounding victories for religion and absolutely no interfaith coalition so inclusive," Dunn said. "Every American is indebted" to Oliver Thomas, who headed the coalition with "energy, skill, grace, and patience."

Thomas had equally high praise for Representative Jack Brooks (D-TX), chair of the House Judiciary Committee that brought the bill to the floor. The House debate yielded staunch, bipartisan support for the measure, with no one speaking in opposition.

Brooks said,

> The Supreme Court's decision three years ago transformed a most hallowed liberty into a mundane concept with little more status than a fishing license—thus subjecting religious freedom to the whims of government officials. That, indeed, has been the sorry legacy of the court's view of this matter.
>
> Passage of this legislation is the only means to restore substance to the constitutional guarantee of religious freedom.

But Dunn warned of premature celebration; he had seen many pieces of legislation suffer a one-chamber-approval death. Without the Senate, the House action would be void.

With Senator Simpson as the lone dissenter, the Senate Judiciary Committee cleared RFRA for consideration by the full chamber on May 6. Levendosky again wrote a column criticizing Simpson, this time as "the first and, to date, the only congressman to vote against RFRA in this session." He continued:

> Last year he killed the act without having heard committee discussion or debate about it. This year he voted against it with vague warnings that "something is wrong with this bill," but he didn't know what—just a feeling.

At the hearing, Simpson said he was concerned that RFRA could create problems in prisons by forcing administrators to accommodate prisoners' religious practice to the detriment of security and order. Others raised the same issue but voted for the bill, saying they might discuss the problem on the floor of the Senate.

Several state attorneys general had expressed concern to the committee that RFRA might have the unintended consequence of upsetting the delicate balance of inmates' rights and prison security. In light of those concerns, the Justice Department reviewed RFRA, and Attorney General Janet Reno remained steadfast in her support of the bill.

She told members of the American Bar Association in an April 30 address that she favored passage of the bill, but her strongest endorsement came in a May 5 letter to committee chair Biden. She urged "swift enactment" without a prison amendment. Reno wrote:

Certainly, the strong interest that prison administrators and society in general have in preserving security, order, and discipline in prison will receive great weight in the determination whether the government meets the compelling interest test. . . . Activities that are presumptively dangerous or carry a demonstrable likelihood of jeopardizing discipline within a prison will continue to be subject to regulation after enactment of S. 578.

Likewise, prison administrators will retain authority, in many instances, to regulate the time, place, and manner of an inmate's exercise of religion.

Despite strong assurances from the administration, the prison issue arose on the Senate floor. Senator Harry Reid (D-NV) introduced an amendment that would exempt prisoners from RFRA, but it was defeated by a 41–58 vote. The final bill was approved 97–3. Ironically, Senator Simpson voted for the bill, whose only detractors were three Baptist senators: Robert Byrd (D-WV), Harlan Mathews (D-TN), and Jesse Helms (R-NC).

Because of minor changes, RFRA was returned to the House for final action; the House unanimously approved the final version on November 3 (see Appendix C). Thirteen days later, President Clinton signed the bill into law during a ceremony on the south lawn of the White House that included more than 200 members of the religious community. Clinton and Vice President Al Gore, both Baptists, lauded the unprecedented coalition's work. Clinton said,

I'm told that, as many of the people in the coalition worked together across ideological and religious lines, some new friendships were formed and some new trust was established, which shows, I suppose, that the power of God is such that even in the legislative process miracles can happen.

Bill signings frequently are routine, he said, but this event had a more majestic quality because it allowed them to reaffirm the historic role that people of faith have played in America. Dunn cited God's grace as the reason the diverse coalition remained intact, and he added that Thomas as the chair was the "instrument of that grace."

Tyrone Pitts, general secretary of the Progressive National Baptist Convention Inc. and former BJC chair, said,

Not since the civil rights struggle has there been a group of religious leaders who have come together to pave the way for a piece of legislation that is more meaningful to us as people of God.

Not only are you to be commended for that act, but we should see this as a signal that God is calling us (the religious community) to move more and more together to make sure religious freedom and the freedom of all persons are guaranteed.

Pointing to the symbolism of a Baptist president signing the bill, Pitts added, "It's a major signal for us to realize that God indeed is moving us in a new direction—in a direction of freedom."

BJC General Counsel Oliver Thomas (right) confers with Edward Kennedy (D-MA) (left) and Orrin Hatch (R-UT), Senate cosponsors of the Religious Freedom Restoration Act, at a March 1993 news conference marking its reintroduction.

President Bill Clinton shares a laugh with fellow Baptists James M. Dunn and Oliver S. Thomas after signing the Religious Freedom Restoration Act during a South Lawn ceremony November 16, 1993.

Chapter 6
The Prodigal Parent

"I believe this notion of the separation of church and state was the figment of some infidel's imagination."

—W. A. Criswell
CBS Evening News
August 23, 1984

"Religious liberty entails the separation of church and state, a principle declared by Jesus himself (Matt 22:21)."

—Herschel H. Hobbs
Arkansas Baptist Newsmagazine
1993

Drug dealers. Anti-Christ. Unchurched. Name the slur, and the staff of the Baptist Joint Committee has heard worse. As part of the hostile takeover of the Southern Baptist Convention, some fundamentalist leaders orchestrated a misinformation campaign to discredit, control, and obliterate the religious liberty agency. The BJC has been familiar with the tactics since the 1950s. In 1953, a staff member of Senator Joseph McCarthy's congressional investigating committee labeled BJC founder Rufus Weaver as a pro-Communist. In an article, the staffer also called Protestant clergymen the "largest single group supporting the Communist apparatus in the United States." The agency opposed McCarthy's tactics in the 1950s and the McCarthyism that infected the nation's largest Protestant denomination in 1979.

Those political tactics ultimately led the SBC to banish the BJC from its ranks. Ironically, the rift occurred not because the BJC failed to adhere to its original SBC mandate, but because it insisted on doing so. In essence, the child was punished for the parent's inconsistency.

The road to the 1991 SBC defunding of the agency began in 1979. A small group of fundamentalists announced a plan to take over the SBC. They would mobilize followers who would elect a president willing to use the office's appointive powers to stack the boards of SBC agencies and institutions with like-minded fundamentalist trustees. By controlling the presidential election, trustees could be handpicked to control SBC employees. The trustees would ensure the employees tow the line; those who did not were fired, harassed, or maligned during the nearly two-decade controversy.

This simple plan seemed untenable in a denomination that claimed more than 14,000,000 members. Most Southern Baptists did not believe a handful of men could topple a denomination built on democratic principles and grassroots polity. But they simply underestimated the tenacity and acumen of the new guard. One of the architects of the takeover, Houston appeals court judge Paul Pressler, described it best in a Baptist Press (BP) article when he said the takeover movement would be "going for the jugular."

In this wider context, the BJC became one of many targets. But frustrated fundamentalists would have to resort to Herculean efforts to discredit the agency when they could not control or manipulate it. They appointed study committees, investigatory bodies, and parallel groups and made repeated attempts to withdraw SBC financial support. They launched intense personal attacks on Executive Director James M. Dunn. They tried scare tactics and intimidation, but the BJC was in a fortunate position of being a joint endeavor that could not be controlled by a single member body. The courageous and steadfast support of those conventions sustained the agency during the controversy and since the SBC defunding.

The BJC and SBC clashed early in the controversy over a constitutional amendment on school prayer. The BJC stuck by the historic Baptist principle opposing government-sponsored prayer. The new SBC power brokers fell in line behind President Ronald Reagan. At the 1982 SBC meeting in New Orleans, messengers adopted a resolution supporting Reagan's amendment—juxtaposing the denomination against the BJC's position and the denomination's previous stance.

A Reagan aide confirmed to BP that the White House encouraged Edward McAteer to urge the SBC to support the amendment. McAteer, founder and president of a new right-wing organization, played a major role in getting the measure through the SBC Resolutions Committee and to the convention floor.

In a BP article, McAteer said he hoped Dunn would "repent." But the BJC and Dunn, championing a tradition dating back at least to Roger Williams and the founding of Rhode Island, refused to do so. Critics said that the BJC ought to reflect the

SBC's new position. In fact, the Kansas-Nebraska Convention of Southern Baptists said the BJC should fall in line or get out.

Observers believed that most of the criticism stemmed from an unholy union of religion and politics. Dunn and the agency were criticized in a January 21, 1983, radio report of the now defunct Moral Majority, a right-wing organization founded by Jerry Falwell. The report went so far as to suggest that the BJC ought to be defunded. Some observers found it peculiar that this political group, with no official connection to the SBC, would call for such action.

In June 1983, the SBC took two important steps. First, messengers adopted a resolution expressing confidence in the U.S. Constitution as an adequate guarantee of religious freedom, leading to speculation that they were backing off the 1982 resolution. Second, the first two SBC fundamentalists, Samuel T. Currin and Albert Lee Smith Jr., were appointed to the BJC board. Currin was a former aide to Senator Jesse Helms (R-NC) and a strong proponent of the school prayer amendment. Smith was a former one-term congressman, who won election with the backing of the Alabama Moral Majority.

Currin and Smith were elected to the SBC Public Affairs Committee, which had representation on the BJC. Although both men came with a known antagonistic agenda, the staff was not overly concerned at first. How much influence could two men have on a forty-five-member board that represented eight conventions in addition to the SBC? Plenty. And their animosity was felt immediately.

John Baker, director of BJC research services, testified against the school prayer amendment before a Senate panel. He pointed to statements by various Baptist bodies, including the 1983 SBC resolution. At the conclusion of Baker's testimony, Senator Strom Thurmond (R-SC), chair of the Senate Judiciary Committee, produced a letter from Currin that contradicted Baker's position. Currin, without consulting the PAC, wrote Thurmond. Pointing to the 1982 resolution, Currin caused confusion on the Hill by falsely conveying that Baker did not represent a Southern Baptist perspective. The BJC staff was stunned; one board member contradicted its position to members of the U.S. Senate. Twelve of the fifteen PAC members later disclaimed the letter and expressed concern that Currin acted independently. But he had drawn a clear battle line.

Urged by Smith, another state convention—Alabama—called for the defunding of the BJC later that year. This time the criticism focused on Dunn's membership on the board of People for the American Way. In January 1984, Dunn declined renomination to the board, but criticism continued.

Despite Dunn's action, the issue of defunding was unavoidable at the 1984 SBC meeting in Kansas City, Missouri. On the opening day of the convention, messengers narrowly defeated, 5,854–5,480, an attempt to defund the agency. At a press conference following the vote, Dunn said he was grateful that Southern Baptists sustained the agency "in the face of this extremely elaborate, carefully orchestrated campaign that has been going on for months and months," according to a BP story.

But repeated attempts to defund the religious liberty agency persisted. The BJC continued to draw fire because of the perception that it opposed a Republican president. In fact, it simply opposed his policies on church-state issues. Reagan, like several presidents before him, had a personal representative at the Vatican but declined to establish full diplomatic relations there. But in 1984, Reagan decided to up the ante; he announced that he would establish full diplomatic ties with the Holy See. Once again, the BJC found itself opposed to a position of a president who was incredibly popular with SBC fundamentalists. The fact that this was a principled position the agency had held since its inception did not seem to matter to agency detractors. For them, politics took precedence over principle.

In 1985 and 1986, the controversy intensified within the committee itself as more SBC fundamentalists were added to the board. However, the overwhelming majority of the committee never wavered from its adherence to principle and support of the beleaguered agency. Messengers to the 1986 SBC voted to refer the annual defunding motion to its Executive Committee for further study. In September of that year, the Executive Committee named a panel to investigate the agency. Pressler was named to the group. In essence, this gave him license to harass.

After one month, the panel chair Gary Young said that the relationship between the SBC and the BJC needed adjustment, noting that if the relationship were working, "our committee would not be in existence."

The investigation included public hearings on the BJC. At one hearing, the agency was bolstered by a surprise appearance by

Senator Mark Hatfield (R-OR). He told the SBC panel that the agency had played a key role in the adoption of the 1984 Equal Access Act, which helps assure students religious expression in public schools.

But after Hatfield finished his statement, Pressler took aim. He "grilled the Joint Committee staff on several points," according to Religious News Service. He criticized Dunn's involvement with People for the American Way, even though he no longer served on its board.

The study committee finally recommended that the SBC continue to relate to the BJC through the PAC. But the panel also recommended that the PAC be retooled to operate separately as well. Young told BP that the SBC relationship would change because the composition and constituency of the PAC would change. And change they did.

At the 1987 SBC annual meeting, messengers voted to adopt the study committee's recommendation, which included encouragement for trustees of the Christian Life Commission to consider opening a Washington office, and referred to the newly constituted PAC a motion to replace expeditiously BJC personnel.

One of the first actions of the newly structured PAC was to break with SBC tradition and policy by endorsing Robert H. Bork's nomination to the U.S. Supreme Court. The endorsement resolution, offered by Les Csorba III of Alexandria, Virginia, who later took a position with the Bush administration, was approved 7–5. Harold C. Bennett, president-treasurer of the SBC Executive Committee, told the group it was breaking Baptist tradition. Lloyd Elder, president of the Southern Baptist Sunday School Board and PAC member, vocalized his opposition for the record.

After the action, the PAC also came under intense criticism by Porter W. Routh, executive secretary-treasurer of the SBC Executive Committee from 1951 to 1979. In a letter to the editor, Routh pointed to a 1976 SBC motion that reaffirmed the SBC's "long tradition of nonendorsement of any political candidate." Routh noted that the PAC's program statement empowered it to "act only on the basis of principles and policies generally accepted by Baptists or in support of official acts and pronouncements of the cooperating conventions."

Routh's letter continued:

> In the past 100 years, Southern Baptists have perhaps been
> more emotionally involved in the campaigns of John F. Ken-
> nedy in 1960 and Al Smith in 1928. Both were Roman
> Catholics, and there was fear that this would be reflected in
> their presidency. In the case of Mr. Kennedy, this was not true.
> In both cases, the Southern Baptist Convention discussed the
> issues involved, but in neither case was the candidate men-
> tioned by name, and in neither case did the Convention urge
> the election of any other candidate by name.

Routh said the issue was not Bork but the improper endorsement.
He concluded,

> It is a sad day when persons who have incomplete knowledge
> of Baptist history or tradition, or the price they have paid for
> religious liberty, make decisions which are in violation of spe-
> cific Southern Baptist Convention actions, and also in violation
> of the principles of separation of church and state which they
> are elected to defend.

Perhaps no public action so crystallized the deep philosophical
differences between the BJC and its Southern Baptist representatives on the PAC.

Another major dispute arose during the reconfigured PAC's
first meeting. The PAC voted to inquire whether the $448,400
allocated by SBC messengers for the BJC would be channeled
through the PAC. PAC members said that the confusion resulted
from its new mandate to act separately from the BJC.

Thomas Pratt, pastor of Calvary Baptist Church, Brighton,
Colorado, moved that the PAC serve as a conduit for the money
and that the BJC should be funded with the PAC's "approval." It
passed 8–2, even though the chair of the SBC fact-finding committee told the PAC that his panel did not recommend changing
the BJC funding mechanism.

Chairman Young, pastor of First Southern Baptist Church,
Phoenix, Arizona, remained quiet following the SBC's adoption
of his committee's recommendations until the summer of 1988
when he granted an interview with the Arizona Baptist newspa-
per. Young told the *Baptist Beacon* that "inerrancy was never an
issue" in the BJC controversy, which "had to do with control politics, personal dislikes, and the application of theology and

scriptural principles." He told the *Beacon* that messengers needed to know when inerrancy was at issue and when it was not.

Young, who declined a second term on the SBC Executive Committee, said that he attended the first PAC meeting to explain his committee's recommendation, and the PAC members were disinterested in his opinions. He commented,

> I felt exceedingly disappointed, heartsick, a bit angry and felt that I had wasted nine months of my life, nine months of my church's precious time in my absence, and thousands and thousands of Cooperative Program dollars.

Another significant action at the PAC's first meeting, held August 20-21, 1987, was the appointment of a BJC staff evaluation committee, responding to the motion that the BJC staff be brought into line with the SBC. Albert Lee Smith was elected its chair. He wrote Dunn, asking for seven separate items that he wanted supplied to his committee within two weeks. They included:

- a breakdown of the 1986–1987 budget and the proposed budget for 1987–1988
- breakdown of the salaries for the past five years of all the staff members, including housing, retirement, protection, and expense allowances
- information about professional memberships of staff members
- itemized list of expense accounts for the past five years
- BJC constitution and bylaws
- names of BJC committees, their members with denominational affiliation, and chair
- copies of correspondence to and from the professional staff for the past three years.

In addition, the PAC wanted to meet with staff members privately to interview them.

An overwhelming majority of BJC board members voted to refuse the request and to evaluate the staff through its own executive committee. Fundamentalists complained that the SBC gave most of the BJC budget and, therefore, was entitled to more privileges, such as the right to interrogate staff members and read their personal and professional correspondence.

Julian H. Pentecost, editor of the *Religious Herald*, wrote in a September 17, 1987, editorial describing the PAC meeting as "disturbing":

> No one can question the fact that the "new" majority of PAC members came to their first meeting with an agreed-upon agenda and moved aggressively to implement it. Confrontation with the BJC in its customary championing of historic Baptist faith and practice—soul competency, local church autonomy, religious liberty, and church-state separation—seems inevitable.

At its September meeting, the SBC Executive Committee appointed a subcommittee to examine the funding-control issue, naming Scott Humphrey, a layman from Alexandria, Virginia, as its chair. Humphrey told BP:

> It seems to me we are dealing with two groups, and we voted one budget. We told the two groups to do a job, but we told them to do it jointly and independently. Both groups want some of the money or all of the money. It seems to me we are dealing with a budget and financial management problem.

In October 1987, the PAC voted to ask the SBC to sever its ties to the BJC. PAC Chair Currin told BP that this proposal was good for the other eight conventions supporting the BJC, because they "really do not want us."

John Binder, executive director of the North American Baptist Convention, said that was not the case. The issue was not the PAC member's reception but their desire to take over, he said in a BP story. Warren Magnuson, a BJC board member representing the Baptist General Conference, told BP that the SBC group decided to disassociate itself from the BJC board before it ever arrived at the meetings.

Several state conventions stood by the BJC. Virginia Baptists designated $3,000 for the beleaguered agency. Texas voted to continue support, without specifying an amount, and New York set aside $500. North Carolina and Missouri also approved resolutions supporting the BJC.

With three different Baptist voices speaking on Capitol Hill— the BJC, PAC, and CLC—confusion arose concerning who had authority to speak and for whom. (Imagine what Abbott and Costello could have done with that material.) SBC leaders began discussing the possibility of merging the PAC and CLC.

In February 1988, the BJC-PAC funding issue reemerged, and again the PAC did not gain the control it wanted. The funding subcommittee noted that no SBC action had called for a change in the way the BJC should be funded, and as a standing committee, the PAC should ask for its own funds. However, the group did recommend that the BJC make its SBC budget requests through the PAC. The SBC Executive Committee declined the PAC's recommendation to cut off ties to the BJC, but it did reduce its annual contribution to the BJC by nearly $50,000.

At this juncture, even Young's disillusionment with the Executive Committee and public revelations about its leaders' motives could not curb the misinformation machine. Too many good Baptists believed what they were told: the BJC was a bastion of liberalism that must be purged.

In 1989, the open warfare on the BJC was escalated to nuclear proportions. At the February meeting of the Executive Committee, four assaults on the agency's budget were spurned, with the BJC sustaining only a 2.05 percent budget cut—the same reduction most SBC entities had to incur that year. But the Executive Committee also approved the creation of a Religious Liberty Commission that would usurp the BJC's place in SBC life. (The establishment of a new agency requires messenger approval at two consecutive conventions.)

The Religious Liberty Commission proposal sent shockwaves through the Baptist body. Many spoke for and against the motion. Several state Baptist paper editors wrote about it. Bob Allen, editor of the *Baptist True Union*, the newsjournal of the Baptist Convention of Maryland/Delaware, called for Southern Baptists to "back off immediately from the proposed" commission. Allen wrote in an August 3, 1989, editorial:

> Southern Baptists would do well not to let their infighting spill into the BJC, to work for consensus instead of control, to work through existing channels instead of churning out new agencies, and to accept defeat with grace instead of threatening to pull funds.

He recommended Southern Baptists follow the lead of Weaver, the man most responsible for the BJC's founding, who discovered that combining various expressions of the Baptist faith had a greater impact on society. Southern Baptists should accentuate "what Baptists have in common, rather than magnifying differences; that could be a cure for Southern Baptists' own internal malady," Allen wrote.

The contentious nature of the proposal prompted SBC President Jerry Vines to ask for a delay in its consideration. The 1989 SBC was scheduled to have an extensive witnessing campaign in conjunction with its meeting in Las Vegas. Vines did not want a rancorous annual meeting but one that promoted evangelism, he said. Vines secured the needed support of Pressler, and the action was delayed.

Despite Vines' call for an evangelistic spirit, some messengers from the convention floor unsuccessfully attempted to withdraw BJC funding. But SBC messengers knew that fundamentalists wanted to settle the BJC issue. And they would not wait long.

In September 1989, Vines urged the Executive Committee to settle the dispute "in a clear-cut, uncomplicated way," according to BP. His plea followed the group's decision to nix the Religious Liberty Commission, designating the convention's religious liberty assignment to the CLC. Vines suggested the Executive Committee publish information that would help messengers understand the issue before them at the 1990 meeting in New Orleans.

The Executive Committee produced a document titled "Some Reasons for the Southern Baptist Convention 1990–1991 Budget Allocation to Support Religious Liberty and Separation of Church and State." The BJC objected to the document. Oliver S. Thomas, BJC general counsel, said it contained "unjustified personal attacks on former and current staff members" and "numerous factual errors." The BJC made a formal request to the chair of the Executive Committee to correct the factual errors, but the request was rebuffed. Thomas wrote:

> The seriousness of their decision is underscored by the fact that the uncorrected document will be presented to the messengers of the Southern Baptist Convention as the rationale for slashing the budget of the Baptist Joint Committee by more than 87 percent and expanding the program assignment of the Christian Life Commission to include religious liberty.
>
> As a result of this action, the vote on these critical issues will be based largely upon false and misleading information.

McCarthy was alive and well.

Again, many state Baptist paper editors—some at great peril—highlighted the Executive Committee's draconian action. Texas *Baptist Standard* Editor Presnall Wood opposed the proposal:

> Given the choice of who will speak for Southern Baptists on religious liberty, messengers to the New Orleans convention should choose the Baptist Joint Committee on Public Affairs.

J. B. Fowler, editor of the *Baptist New Mexican,* called the defunding "a major mistake and a terribly costly blunder."

Again, Maryland/Delaware's Allen made an eloquent plea on the BJC's behalf. He wrote:

> If you are looking for any consistent logic as to why Southern Baptists need three religious liberty voices instead of one or to why increasing Southern Baptist clout in Washington seems to be emerging as the single most important priority for the Executive Committee, you won't find it. What is at play is a convoluted scheme to keep all the political bases covered until an ultimate goal of punishing the BJCPA is achieved.
>
> Why must the BJC be punished? Essentially because in its fifty-three-year-old relationship with the SBC, the agency's board of trustees took one position in open conflict with a non-binding SBC resolution on school prayer. . . . Beyond that, the BJC has not been—well—Republican enough for a new crop of SBC leaders enamored with the Moral Majority and other right-wing religio-political groups proliferating in the nation's capital.

In New Orleans, messengers followed the Executive Committee's recommendation to reduce by $341,796 their annual contribution to the BJC, leaving SBC support at $50,000. The $50,000 would allow SBC representation on the BJC board. For many convention moderates, the 1990 convention marked a clear victory for fundamentalists. Many moderates left New Orleans never to return to SBC annual meetings.

The next year the SBC voted to cut all funds to the BJC, severing the formal relationship. Ironically, the majority of the BJC staff were Southern Baptists, and the repudiation by their convention stung hard. The SBC no longer wanted Southern Baptists of their kind, period.

But that devastating reality could not dissuade BJC staff from their belief that most Southern Baptists—as individuals—still supported absolute religious liberty for all citizens. In New Orleans, Dunn predicted that individuals and state conventions, many of whom had supported the agency during the controversy, would not let the BJC die. They would make up the short fall, he predicted. History has proved Baptists worthy of such confidence.

Chapter 7
The Next Sixty

"This week, the SBC also cut off all funding for the Baptist Joint Committee on Public Affairs, which has been the nation's leading religious lobby on behalf of church-state separation. Fortunately, however, the committee will continue to do its good work. The difference has been more than made up by Baptist organizations that continue to hew to traditional Baptist principles."

—The Atlanta Constitution
Editorial, June 7, 1991

History is replete with irony, and the Baptist Joint Committee's past is no exception. Among the most ironic pages out of its annals include the Southern Baptist Convention's defunding. What could be more ironic than one group of Baptists punishing another group of Baptists for—of all things—being Baptist? Perhaps just one thing—the greatest irony in BJC history is that the agency achieved its finest accomplishments during its most perilous period. The battle for the Equal Access Act was engaged just before the time the SBC Executive Committee sought to replace the BJC staff. The Religious Freedom Restoration Act became a reality in the aftermath of the SBC defunding. While the agency fought in the halls of Congress to ensure religious liberty for every citizen, it also struggled to keep its doors open.

The survival of the agency, which lost more than 50 percent of its budget on one day, was no small feat. But the credit does not belong to the staff alone. Two factors contributed to the agency's endurance: God's providence and the faithfulness of Baptists who adhered to their principles and traditions.

After the SBC withdrew financial support, several Southern Baptist state conventions, local churches, and individuals contributed funds to the agency. During 1990–1991, individuals giving to the agency jumped from 465 to 715, while the number of contributing churches more than doubled from 135 to 304. Various state conventions, ranging in size from Texas to New England, have given budgeted support since the defunding. But fundamentalists' infiltration in some supportive states, such as Maryland/Delaware, resulted in their eventual withdrawal of funds from the BJC. By 1996, only three state conventions—Texas, Virginia, and North Carolina—were sending monies directly to the religious liberty agency.

Also, the agency's other supporting bodies helped make up the difference. Those groups included: the Alliance of Baptists; American Baptist Churches in the USA; Baptist General Conference; Cooperative Baptist Fellowship; National Baptist Convention of America; National Baptist Convention, USA, Inc.; National Missionary Baptist Convention; North American Baptist Conference; Progressive National Baptist Convention, Inc.; Religious Liberty Council; and Seventh-Day Baptist General Conference.

The BJC bolstered its development efforts, looking for new sources of revenue. The agency implemented austerity measures. During this financial duress, the agency managed to survive without laying off a single staff member or failing to meet payroll.

As the agency struggled to restore religious liberty to its rightful place and pay its bills, it faced another nemesis. Some SBC leaders seemed unsatisfied with the excommunication of the BJC. Nothing short of the agency's demise would satisfy them. Or so it appeared. Some even speculated that one of the unwritten program assignments of the CLC's Washington office was to try to discredit the BJC. An unhealthy rivalry between the two emerged.

One of the most visible aspects of this conflict involved the agencies' news services. The BJC had housed the Washington Bureau of Baptist Press (BP) for decades under the direction of BJC communicators Barry Garrett, Stan Hastey, Kathy Palen, and Larry Chesser. But with the opening of the CLC office in Washington, the bureau came under dispute. BP head Herb Hollinger voiced a willingness to compromise, but those with more power would not have it. The bureau was yanked from the BJC and placed in the CLC.

Anticipating the move, the BJC already had established Baptist News Service as its own independent news operation. When the BP bureau was pulled, BNS began operating informally as the Washington bureau of Associated Baptist Press (ABP). ABP is an independent Baptist news source established after the SBC Executive Committee, meeting behind locked doors and armed guards, fired BP editors Al Shackleford and Dan Martin without giving cause.

But the news service was not the only matter of dispute between the two agencies. Conflict arose when the CLC laid claim to the BJC's main financial asset—nearly $400,000 on deposit at the Southern Baptist Foundation. In 1964, SBC messengers authorized capital funds for public affairs. At the time, the terms Public Affairs Committee, Joint Committee on Public Affairs, and Baptist Joint Committee on Public Affairs were used interchangeably. All the terms reflected name changes for the one agency that had represented Southern Baptists for five decades. The account, held in trust at the Southern Baptist Foundation in the BJC's name, had been under its control for decades.

Messengers to the 1964 convention set aside the funds for office space. The agency used the interest from the original $300,000 fund to pay rent. Over the years, the BJC earned more than $600,000 in interest.

In 1991, the agency signed a contract on a building and asked for the money to help purchase it. But the SBC seized the account, claiming that the money had been set aside for public affairs and the BJC no longer represented public affairs on behalf of Southern Baptists. The SBC decided to reallocate those funds to the CLC.

Unwilling to relinquish its account, the BJC began negotiations with SBC leaders to avoid a legal suit. The BJC, which had secured the law firm of Powell, Goldstein, Frazer, and Murphy to retain its funds if necessary, extended an offer to use Christian conciliation to settle the dispute. Eventually, the two sides reached an amicable agreement without going to court. The BJC received about $80,000 capital appreciation plus $100,000 in four installments. The remaining portion was allocated to the CLC.

With a competing agency and no SBC-backing, the BJC faced tough questions about its viability. The speculation was unavoidable: Would the BJC limp along in survival mode? Or would it continue to make a real impact?

The record speaks for itself. In recent years, the BJC has:

• Chaired the coalition of religious and educational groups that revised the guidelines for implementing the Equal Access Act after it was upheld by the Supreme Court. The guidelines have been distributed to all school districts in the country for their secondary school principals.

• Co-authored and co-sponsored the nation's first comprehensive curriculum for teaching about religion in public schools.

• Co-sponsored a major conference celebrating the bicentennial of the Bill of Rights.

• Chaired a committee of religious group attorneys that meets periodically with the commissioner of the IRS to resolve problems on churches and tax policy.

• Spearheaded the Coalition for the Free Exercise of Religion that provided the primary support for RFRA, which was signed into law November 16, 1993.

• Worked to ensure that military personnel in the Persian Gulf were allowed to receive Bibles and other religious literature for personal use through the mail.

• Advocated that the U.S. Supreme Court maintain governmental neutrality toward religion in several key cases.

• Continued to fight parochial aid battles, now debated under the guise of "school choice" proposals.

• Organized an inaugural eve prayer service January 19, 1993, at First Baptist Church in Washington for President Bill Clinton and Vice President Al Gore—both Southern Baptists. The event, attended by the Clintons, the Gores, the Carters, and TV commentator Bill Moyers, drew 1,000 Baptists.

• Helped produce "A Shared Vision: Religious Liberty in the Twenty-First Century" and presented it to Gore (Appendix D).

• Helped produce "A Joint Statement of Current Law" as a guide for the recurring public school prayer debate (Appendix E).

• Helped countless Baptists on an individual basis. For example, BJC attorney J. Brent Walker helped a Virginia pastor avoid a subpoena to testify in a criminal trial about facts he obtained during confidential counseling. The BJC general counsel's office also provides free advice on a variety of issues, including questions regarding church liability and the tax-exempt status of their churches.

Although the Baptist bodies supporting the agency and its staff have changed, the BJC has not. From Rufus Weaver to James Dunn, the BJC has maintained that both church and state benefit when neither does the other's job.

Despite the sixty-year vigil at Mr. Jefferson's wall, challenges to religious liberty continue. As the new century approaches, the BJC recommits itself to another watch to ensure that every citizen is free to worship or not to worship according to the dictates of conscience.

Appendix A
The American Baptist Bill of Rights

[This pronouncement on religious liberty was unanimously approved at the 1939 annual sessions of the Southern Baptist Convention (May 20), the Northern Baptist Convention (June 21), and the National Baptist Convention (September 7). The Associated Committees on Public Relations, representing those conventions, published and copyrighted the document in 1940.]

A PRONOUNCEMENT UPON RELIGIOUS LIBERTY

No issue in modern life is more urgent or more complicated than the relation of organized religion to organized society. The sudden rise of the European dictators to power has changed fundamentally the organic law of the governments through which they exercise sovereignty, and as a result, the institutions of religion are either suppressed or made subservient to the ambitious national programs of these new totalitarian states.

FOUR THEORIES OF THE RELATION OF CHURCH AND STATE

There are four conceptions of the relation of church and state:

(1) The church is above the state, a theory held by those who claim that their ecclesiastical head is the vicar of Christ on earth.
(2) The church is alongside of the state, a theory held by the state churches of various countries.
(3) The state is above the church, a theory held by the totalitarian governments.
(4) The church is separate from the state, championed by the Baptists everywhere, and held by those governments that have written religious liberty into their fundamental law.

BAPTISTS OPENED THE DOOR OF RELIGIOUS LIBERTY

Three hundred years have passed since the establishment under Baptist leadership of the first civil government in which full religious liberty was granted to the citizens forming the compact. The original document, preserved in the city hall, Providence, Rhode Island, is a covenant of citizens: "We, whose names are hereunder, desirous to inhabit in the town of Providence, do promise to subject ourselves in active or passive obedience to all such orders or agreements as shall be made for public good for the body in an orderly way, by the major assent of the present inhabitants, masters of families, incorporated together into a town fellowship, and such others whom they shall admit unto themselves, only in civil things." These four concluding words opened wide the door to religious liberty.

PROVIDED AN ASYLUM FOR THE PERSECUTED

This document was written three hundred years ago by Roger Williams, a Baptist minister and a student under Lord Coke, who had been banished from the colony of Massachusetts for his espousal of the freedom of conscience. The founder of a civil commonwealth called the Providence Plantations, he started a political movement which made the colony of Rhode Island the asylum of the persecuted and the home of the free.

LAID THE FOUNDATIONS OF RELIGIOUS LIBERTY

The Baptists of England through Leonard Busher had in 1614 pleaded with James I for freedom of conscience. Roger Williams became the apostle of religious liberty in colonial America. Dr. John Clarke, the pastor of the Baptist church of Newport, Rhode Island, as agent of the Rhode Island Colony and Providence Plantations, secured from Charles II in 1663 a charter in which the religious liberty claimed by the colonists was guaranteed through a royal decree. For the first time in the history of the world, a civil government was founded that guaranteed to its inhabitants absolute religious freedom.

PLEADED FOR THE RELIGIOUS RIGHTS OF ALL MEN

The Baptists of the colony of Virginia where, between 1767 and 1778, forty-two Baptist ministers were jailed for preaching the gospel, through repeated memorials pleaded with the authorities for religious liberty. Favored by the leadership of Thomas Jefferson, James Madison, George Mason, John Leland, and other lovers of freedom, they secured the free exercise of religion through the passage of the Statute Establishing Religious Freedom in 1786. Not content with the winning of religious equality in Virginia, Baptists scrutinized the terms of the federal Constitution and were largely instrumental in securing the passage of the First Amendment, which declares that "Congress shall make no law respecting an establishment of religion, or prohibiting the free exercise thereof." As to this, see the letter of George Washington to the Baptists of Virginia.

Religious liberty, as our Baptist forefathers defined it, was an emancipation from governmental and all other coercive restrictions that thwarted the free exercise of religion and the high purpose to achieve a Christlike character.

BAPTISTS STRESS SPIRITUALITY

The principles that animate the activities of the Baptists, principles which they hold clearly to be taught in the New Testament, are the worth of the individual; the necessity of the new birth; the preservation of Christian truth in Christian symbols; spirituality, or the free pursuit of Christian piety; the persuading of others through personal testimony, by the life of example, the preaching of the gospel, and the creation of Christian institutions, to the end that the unbelieving will be reconciled to God through a personal faith in Jesus Christ; the organization of groups of obedient believers into churches of Christ, democratic in the processes and theocratic in the principles of their government, and the continued uplifting of human society through the spirit of Christ and the ideals of his kingdom, having as its final objective the establishment of the eternal, unchanging purpose of Almighty God in the hearts of men and the institutions of mankind.

AFFIRM THE COMPETENCY OF
THE HUMAN SOUL IN RELIGION

The conception of the dignity of the individual, as held by Baptists, is grounded in the conviction that every soul possesses the capacity and the inalienable right to deal with God for himself, and to deprive any soul of his right of direct access to God is to usurp the prerogatives of the individual and the function of God.

FREE CHURCHES WITHIN A FREE STATE

Standing as we do for the principle of voluntariness in religion, grounded upon the competency of the human soul, Baptists are essentially antagonistic to every form of religious coercion or persecution. We admit to our membership only those who give evidence that they are regenerated, but we recognize gladly that the grace of God is not limited to those who apply to us, and that our spiritual fellowship embraces all who have experienced the new birth and are walking in newness of life, by whatever name they may be called. We hold that the church of Christ, which in the Bible is called "the body of Christ," is not to be identified with any denomination or church that seeks to exercise ecclesiastical authority, but includes all the regenerated whoever and wherever they are, as these are led by the Holy Spirit. This church is a body without formal organization, and therefore cannot enter into contractual relations on any basis with the state. For this reason, Baptists believe in free churches within a free state.

TODAY BAPTISTS FEEL CONSTRAINED
TO DECLARE THEIR POSITION

Since every session of the Congress considers legislation that raises the question as to the relation of the federal government to the institutions and the agencies of religion, and since recently many tendencies have appeared that involve the freedom of religion and conscience, and furthermore, since there are some state constitutions which do not have embodied in them the Bill of Rights of the federal Constitution, American Baptists feel constrained to declare their position and their convictions.

THE TREND TOWARD PATERNALISM

Today the trend of government, even in democratic countries, lies in the direction of greater centralization. The philanthropic activities of the churches within the United States are being taken over by the government. The defective, the indigent, and the dependent groups of our social order have long been supported from public funds. The greatest charity agency on earth today is our federal government. More and more the people are looking to the state to provide. As a nation we are becoming paternalistic. Efforts are now being made to place in the hands of the government the pensioning of those who are employed by the churches and the agencies that serve them, to grant to sectarian schools financial aid from tax-raised funds, and to support from public funds institutions that are established and managed by sectarian bodies.

BAPTISTS CONDEMN THE UNION OF CHURCH AND STATE

Baptists hold that the coercion of religious bodies through special taxes, the use of tax-raised funds for sectarian schools, and the appropriation of public money to institutions created to extend the power and influence of any religious body, violate the spirit of the First Amendment and result in the union of state and church.

OPPOSE SPECIAL FAVORS EXTENDED
TO ANY ECCLESIASTICAL BODY

We oppose the establishing of diplomatic relations with any ecclesiastical body, the extension of special courtesies by our government to any ecclesiastical official as such, and the employment of any of the branches of our national defense in connection with religious services that are held to honor any ecclesiastical leader. All such violations of principle must be resisted in their beginnings.

CITIZENS OF TWO COMMONWEALTHS

We acknowledge ourselves to be citizens of two commonwealths, one earthly, the United States, the other heavenly, the Kingdom of God; and we claim the right to be good citizens of both. We recognize the sovereignty of the state, and we give allegiance to the state, but we cannot give to the state the control of our consciences. We must obey God rather than men.

The government resorts to coercion; we use persuasion. The government has authority over the acts of its citizens; we have to do with the motives. The business of the government is to make good laws; our business is to make good citizens who continue to demand the enactment of better laws, embodying higher and still higher ethical standards. The end of governmental administration is equal justice under law. The end of our endeavor is the establishment of the will of God in the hearts and institutions of men. If one of us accepts an office in the government, he recognizes it not only as a public trust, but also as a divine entrustment; for the powers that be are ordained of God. In a democracy like ours, it is possible to be a loyal American and a devoted Christian. This is true because religious liberty is an essential part of our fundamental law.

DEFENDERS OF RELIGIOUS LIBERTY

Believing religious liberty to be not only an inalienable human right, but indispensable to human welfare, a Baptist must exercise himself to the utmost in the maintenance of absolute religious liberty for his Jewish neighbor, his Catholic neighbor, his Protestant neighbor, and for everybody else. Profoundly convinced that any deprivation of this right is a wrong to be challenged, Baptists condemn every form of compulsion in religion or restraint of the free consideration of the claims of religion. We stand for a civil state, "with full liberty in religious concernments."

Appendix B
The Equal Access Act
(Public Law 98-377)

DENIAL OF EQUAL ACCESS PROHIBITED

Sec. 4071.

(a) It shall be unlawful for any public secondary school which receives federal financial assistance and which has a limited open forum to deny equal access or a fair opportunity to, or discriminate against, any students who wish to conduct a meeting within that limited open forum on the basis of the religious, political, philosophical, or other content of the speech at such meetings.

(b) A public secondary school has a limited open forum whenever such school grants an offering to or opportunity for one or more noncurriculum related student groups to meet on school premises during noninstructional time.

(c) Schools shall be deemed to offer a fair opportunity to students who wish to conduct a meeting within its limited open forum if such school uniformly provides that—
   (1) the meeting is voluntary and student-initiated;
   (2) there is no sponsorship of the meeting by the school, the government, or its agents or employees;
   (3) employees or agents of the school or government are present at religious meetings only in a nonparticapatory capacity;
   (4) the meeting does not materially and substantially interfere with the orderly conduct of educational activities within the school; and
   (5) nonschool persons may not direct, conduct, control, or regularly attend activities of student groups.

(d) Nothing in this subchapter shall be construed to authorize the United States or any state or political subdivision thereof—
   (1) to influence the form or content of any prayer or other religious activity;
   (2) to require any person to participate in prayer or other religious activity;
   (3) to expend public funds beyond the incidental cost of providing the space for student-initiated meetings;
   (4) to compel any school agent or employee to attend a school meeting if the content of the speech at the meeting is contrary to the beliefs of the agent or employee;
   (5) to sanction meetings that are otherwise unlawful;
   (6) to limit the rights of groups of students which are not of a specified numerical size; or
   (7) to abridge the constitutional rights of any person.

(e) Notwithstanding the availability of any other remedy under the Constitution or the laws of the United States, nothing in this subchapter shall be construed to authorize the United States to deny or withhold federal financial assistance to any school.

(f) Nothing in this subchapter shall be construed to limit the authority of the school, its agents or employees, to maintain order and discipline on school premises, to protect the well-being of students and faculty, and to assure that attendance of students at meetings is voluntary.

DEFINITIONS

Sec. 4072.

As used in this subchapter—

(1) The term "secondary school" means a public school which provides secondary education as determined by state law.

(2) The term "sponsorship" includes the act of promoting, leading, or participating in a meeting. The assignment of a teacher, administrator, or other school employee to a meeting for custodial purposes does not constitute sponsorship of the meeting.

(3) The term "meeting" includes those activities of student groups which are permitted under a school's limited open forum and are not directly related to the school curriculum.

(4) The term "noninstructional time" means time set aside by the school before actual classroom instruction begins or after actual classroom instruction ends.

SEVERABILITY

Sec. 4073. If any provision of this subchapter or the application thereof to any person or circumstances is judicially determined to be invalid, the provisions of the remainder of the subchapter and the application to other persons or circumstances shall not be affected thereby.

CONSTRUCTION

Sec. 4074. The provisions of this subchapter shall supersede all other provisions of federal law that are inconsistent with the provisions of this subchapter.

Appendix C
The Religious Freedom Restoration Act
(Public Law 103-141)

Congressional findings and declaration of purposes.

(a) Findings

The Congress finds that—

(1) the framers of the Constitution, recognizing free exercise of religion as an unalienable right, secured its protection in the First Amendment to the Constitution;

(2) laws "neutral" toward religion may burden religious exercise as surely as laws intended to interfere with religious exercise;

(3) governments should not substantially burden religious exercise without compelling justification;

(4) in *Employment Division v. Smith*, 494 U.S. 872 (1990), the Supreme Court virtually eliminated the requirement that the government justify burdens on religious exercise imposed by laws neutral toward religion; and

(5) the compelling interest test as set forth in prior federal court rulings is a workable test for striking sensible balances between religious liberty and competing prior governmental interests.

(b) Purposes

The purposes of this act are—

(1) to restore the compelling interest test as set forth in *Sherbert v. Verner*, 374 U.S. 398 (1963) and *Wisconsin v. Yoder*, 406 U.S. 205 (1972) and to guarantee its application in all cases where free exercise of religion is substantially burdened; and

(2) to provide a claim or defense to persons whose religious exercise is substantially burdened by government.

Free exercise of religion protected.

(a) In general—

Government shall not substantially burden a person's exercise of religion even if the burden results from a rule of general applicability, except as provided in subsection (b).

(b) Exception—

Government may substantially burden a person's exercise of religion only if it demonstrates that application of the burden to the person—

(1) is in furtherance of a compelling governmental interest; and

(2) is the least restrictive means of furthering that compelling governmental interest.

(c) Judicial relief—
A person whose religious exercise has been burdened in violation of this section may assert that violation as a claim or defense in a judicial proceeding and obtain appropriate relief against a government. Standing to assert a claim or defense under this section shall be governed by the general rules of standing under Article III of the Constitution.

Attorneys fees.
(a) Judicial proceedings—
Section 722 of the Revised Statutes (42 U.S.C. 1988) is amended by inserting "the Religious Freedom Restoration Act of 1993," before "or title VI of the Civil Rights Act of 1964".
(b) Administrative proceedings—
Section 504(b)(1)(C) of title 5, United States Code, is amended—
(1) by striking "and" at the end of clause (ii);
(2) by striking the semicolon at the end of clause (iii) and inserting ", and"; and
(3) by inserting "(iv) the Religious Freedom Restoration Act of 1993;" after clause (iii).

Definitions.
As used in this act—
(1) the term "government" includes a branch, department, agency, instrumentality, and official (or other person acting under color of law) of the United States, a state, or a subdivision of a state;
(2) the term "state" includes the District of Columbia, the Commonwealth of Puerto Rico, and each territory and possession of the United States;
(3) the term "demonstrates" means meets the burdens of going forward with the evidence and of persuasion; and
(4) the term "exercise of religion" means the exercise of religion under the First Amendment to the Constitution.

Applicability.
(a) In general—
This act applies to all federal and state law, and the implementation of that law, whether statutory or otherwise, and whether adopted before or after the enactment of this act.
(b) Rule of construction—
Federal statutory law adopted after the date of the enactment of this act is subject to this act unless such law explicitly excludes such application by reference to this act.

(c) Religious belief unaffected—
   Nothing in this act shall be construed to authorize any government to burden any religious belief.

Establishment clause unaffected.
   Nothing in this act shall be construed to affect, interpret, or in any way address that portion of the First Amendment prohibiting laws respecting the establishment of religion (referred to in this section as the "establishment clause"). Granting government funding, benefits, or exemptions, to the extent permissible under the establishment clause, shall not constitute a violation of this act. As used in this section, the term "granting," used with respect to government funding, benefits, or exemptions, does not include the denial of government funding, benefits, or exemptions.
   Approved November 16, 1993.

Appendix D
A Shared Vision
Religious Liberty in the Twenty-First Century

We join in issuing this statement at a time when America has reaffirmed its commitment to religious freedom through the Religious Freedom Restoration Act and is again recognizing the vital moral and spiritual role religion plays in both our public and private lives.

Yet, at the same time, we are confronted by two strikingly different views about the proper role of religion in public life. One portrays America as a Christian or Judeo-Christian nation. This view wrongly suggests that the Founders never meant to separate the institutions of church and state or to prohibit the establishment of religion. Such a view is historically inaccurate and endangers our common welfare because it uses religion to divide rather than unite the American people. This view of religion in public life, inaccurate and dangerous as it is, has gained credence in reaction to another inaccurate and equally damaging view of the proper role of religion in public life. The other view sees religion and religious groups as having a minimal role in—perhaps even being barred from—the vital public discourses we carry on as a democracy. It sees faith-based involvement in the democratic process as violating the principle of church-state separation. It regards religious arguments as naive and seeks to embarrass any who profess religious motivation for their public positions on political issues. This view denies our country the powerful moral guidance of our religious heritage and discourages many of our brightest and most committed citizens from actively participating in our public life.

As individuals and organizations committed to religious liberty as well as a robust role for religion in public life, we share a different vision about the future: a vision that avoids both the theocratic tendencies on one side and the hostility toward religion associated with the other. Now more than ever, the United States must maintain its commitment to freedom for persons of all faiths or none. We are beset by religious and ethnic conflict abroad. Exploding pluralism challenges us at home. At such a time, we must reaffirm our dedication to providing what Roger Williams called a "haven for the cause of conscience." We agree with Williams that conscience is best guarded by maintaining a healthy distance between the institutions of religion and government.

But it is not enough to reaffirm these truths. We must incorporate them into our private lives as well as into our public policies. This statement is a call to action. We must apply these principles in practical ways whether we are electing a school board member or the President, whether we are debating aid to parochial schools or prayer in public schools.

The Constitution

"Congress shall make no law respecting an establishment of religion, or prohibiting the free exercise thereof."

The first sixteen words of the First Amendment form the backbone of the American experiment. Together they guarantee religious liberty for Americans of every faith as well as for those who affirm no faith at all. A profound belief in the free exercise of religion motivated the decision of the Founders to disestablish religion in the new nation. The connecting link between the two clauses is freedom of conscience.

While not divorcing religion from public life, the establishment clause separates the institutions of church and state. Grounded in the belief that (1) government should serve all citizens regardless of their religious belief or disbelief and (2) authentic faith must be free and voluntary, the separation of church and state has been good for religion. This "lively experiment" has allowed American religions to flourish with unparalleled strength and diversity. The religious and ethnic diversity of the United States makes the constitutional prohibition against laws respecting an establishment of religion more important than ever. No one wants government taking sides against their religion in favor of someone else's. That principle cuts both ways. In matters of faith, government must not take sides at all.

Critics of the establishment clause argue that the phrase "separation of church and state" does not appear in the Constitution and that society cannot survive without government support of religion. As to the former, they are correct. "Separation of church and state," like "separation of powers," "fair trial," or even "religious freedom," does not appear in the Constitution. Yet, Article VI's prohibition against religious tests for public office and the establishment clause's prohibition against laws even "respecting" an establishment of religion make clear that government is to be neutral in matters of faith. As to the latter, government support has proven a hindrance, not a help, to religion. History is replete with wrecked governments and wrecked churches brought down by the unhealthy union of church and state.

Some suggest that government support for religion should be permitted as long as no religion is favored over another and no citizen is forced to participate. The weight of the evidence suggests the Framers considered and rejected this approach. Even benign, noncoercive endorsements of religion make outsiders of those who are nonadherents of the prevailing faith. A proper interpretation of the establishment clause ensures that one's standing in the political community is not affected by one's standing in the religious community.

In practical terms, the separation of church and state requires that government refrain from promoting or inhibiting religion. Neutrality—by which religion is accommodated but never advocated by the state—should be the touchstone for interpreting both religion clauses.

The free exercise clause was designed to safeguard the inalienable right of Americans to believe, worship, and practice any faith we may choose without government interference. Subsumed in this right is the freedom to change our religious beliefs as we may see fit and to live according to our individual and communal beliefs. All faiths must be free to order their own internal affairs without governmental intrusion. No faith can ever be prohibited, penalized or declared heretical by the government. All must be equally secure, minority as well as majority.

Like most constitutional rights, the free exercise of religion is not absolute. It cannot extend to practices that harm other human beings or threaten public safety and welfare. Absent some compelling reason, however, government should not be able to restrict religious exercise.

The free exercise clause can be only as vital and vibrant as the spirit of liberty abroad in the land. If that spirit is squelched or submerged, for whatever reason, the rights and freedoms of all citizens are at risk. In the words of the 1688 Williamsburg charter: "A right for one is a right for another—and a responsibility for all."

Unfortunately, the Supreme Court's enforcement of the free exercise clause has been uneven over the years. While the Court has frequently reaffirmed the value of full and robust religious expression, it has occasionally failed to protect these important principles when faced with claims by unpopular or politically weak groups. For some, the protections promised under the free exercise clause have been all too fleeting.

Tragically, the Supreme Court's decision in *Employment Division v. Smith* (1990) weakened the free exercise clause even further. Describing the traditional legal protections for religion as a "luxury," the Court rolled back a half century of legal precedent. After *Smith*, the government in most cases was no longer required to demonstrate a compelling reason for restricting religious exercise.

Smith has been applied in dozens of free exercise cases around the country. The regrettable—though not unexpected—result has been that the citizen has lost almost every one of these cases. Orthodox Jews and Hmongs have been subjected to mandatory autopsies, violating their deeply held religious beliefs. Evangelical churches have been zoned out of commercial areas, severely impeding their ability to worship. Churches have been subjected to historical landmarking laws as local governments attempted to dictate the configuration of their buildings. The rights of prisoners to freely exercise their religion have been routinely denied. After *Smith*, our "first liberty" was not only no longer first; it was barely a liberty.

We applaud the passage of the Religious Freedom Restoration Act, which restores the protections for religious liberty stripped away by *Smith*. Thankfully, our system of checks and balances allows Congress to enact laws providing more protection for the exercise of religion than was recognized by the Supreme Court in *Smith*. Still, we long for the day when the Court again recognizes the exercise of religion as a fundamental constitutional right entitled to the highest level of legal protection.

Religion and Politics

As concerned citizens, religious people should and do seek public office. As a conscience in society, religious organizations should and do seek to influence public policy. Separation of church and state does not mean the separation of religion and politics or, for that matter, of God and government.

While religious groups serve an important role in holding government accountable for its actions, that role can be maintained only when religion maintains a healthy distance from government.

Any attempt at affecting public policy should be tempered by a tolerance for differing views and a recognition that a multiplicity of voices is crucial for the success of a democratic society. Neither church nor state may control, dominate, or subjugate the other. Article VI of the Constitution wisely provides that no religious test shall be required for public office. Portraying America as a "Christian nation" violates the American commitment to both democratic government and religious liberty. Where religion is concerned, no person should be made to feel an outcast in his or her own land.

Accordingly, we must:
• Defend the right of religious individuals and organizations to speak, debate, and advocate openly in the public square
• Stand firm by the principle that government action with a primary purpose or effect that advances religion violates the separation of church and state.

Similarly, we should:
• Discourage efforts to make a candidate's religious affiliation or non-affiliation a campaign issue
• Discourage candidates from invoking divine authority for their policies and platforms or from characterizing their opponents as sinful or ungodly.

Religion and Public Education

One of the most critical issues facing our country is how best to educate our children. While recognizing the usefulness of private education, we affirm the particular importance of the public school system in accomplishing that task. Public schools belong to all citizens regardless of their faith perspectives. Public schools have the difficult task of equipping children for citizenship and transmitting to them our civic values.

The primary goal of the public schools is the education of children in an increasingly diverse society, not to provide a captive audience for the transmission of sectarian values. As a result, schools must not allow the public trust to be manipulated for religious goals. Schools are not to sponsor any religious exercises or to allow religious ceremonies at school-directed events. Public schools must remain neutral toward religion. As agents of the state, they must not promote or endorse any religion, or even religion in general. Nevertheless, public schools should accommodate the religious rights of students when that can be done without disrupting the learning process or interfering with the rights of others.

Applying these general principles, schools may teach about religion so long as it is accomplished from an academic, objective perspective that eschews all forms of proselytizing. Teaching about religion should occur when the subject naturally arises in the curriculum. We oppose interjecting religious beliefs into the curriculum at inappropriate points, such as attempting to teach creationism in biology class under the guise of science. Schools may not sponsor or encourage prayer or other devotional activities in the public classroom. They should not take sides in religious disputes or suggest one religious tradition is superior to others. They should not teach in a way that undermines the student's sense of citizenship because he or she does not conform to a prescribed religious norm.

Nevertheless, schools should accommodate the free exercise rights of students. Private devotion or religious exercise on the part of the students, including private prayer, Bible reading, or other religious activities, is permitted so long as they do not interfere with other students' rights or with the educational process. Schools should not discourage students from discussing their faith with other students except for reasonable time, place, and manner restrictions. While some of us disagree on the advisability of doing so, schools are generally free, under Supreme Court precedent, to permit a voluntary student religious group to meet and to allow release-time programs off campus for religious studies without academic credit.

In sum, public schools should not advance religion, but should accommodate the free exercise of religion. They may not confer a benefit on religion but may lift governmentally imposed burdens on the free exercise of religion. They may not promote a religious perspective but may protect the religious exercise of students.

Aid to Religious Institutions

We agree with Jefferson and Madison that it is wrong to tax citizens to support the teaching of religion. In the words of the Virginia Statute for Establishing Religious Freedom: "No man shall be compelled to frequent or support any religious worship, place, or ministry whatsoever." Therefore, we oppose direct or indirect government funding of parochial schools at primary and secondary levels and of pervasively sectarian colleges and universities.

On the other hand, government aid to certain social service programs sponsored by religious organizations, such as homes for children and the elderly and hospitals, enjoys a long history. Aid to religious institutions that provide manifestly secular services (e.g., hospitals) does not pose a threat to religious liberty, if services are provided on a nondiscriminatory basis. However, if an institution indoctrinates its clients with religion, or discriminates based on religion in its admission policies, it should be deemed ineligible for government aid.

Some services are at the margins between education and social services and may require safeguards to protect church-state separation. Other questions arise when funded social services (e.g., foster homes or homes for the elderly) are residential in nature. In such cases government must arrange for residents' religious needs to be met, where possible, through access to existing ministries in the community.

Several broad and uniting principles should be applied in determining when it is appropriate for religious social services providers to receive government aid. Reference should be made to the types of institutions and services involved; the constituency to whom the services are provided; and the adequacy of church-state safeguards. Further, government's partnership with religious institutions for purposes of facilitating the availability of social services should recognize the nonfunded programs in those institutions need not operate under the same standards as publicly funded programs. Religious institutions receiving governmental funds for secular programs should be permitted, consistent with constitutional principles, to maintain their religious identities.

Conclusion

Our heritage of religious liberty and church-state separation must be reaffirmed. The increasing religious pluralism in our country beckons us to turn this heritage into a legacy. The aspirations of the Founders—that religion should involve a voluntary response and that government should remain neutral toward religion—must be converted into practical reality. Daniel Carroll of Maryland said it well over 200 years ago when he declared that "the rights of conscience are . . . of particular delicacy and will little bear the gentlest touch of governmental hand." Carroll's lofty view of conscience captures our understanding of our past and guides our vision of the future. We commit ourselves to making this ideal a reality as we approach the twenty-first century.

Al Albergate
The Rev. Dr. Jimmy R. Allen
Mimi Alperin
*American Jewish Committee
*American Jewish Congress
*Americans for Religious Liberty
*Americans United for Separation
    of Church and State
Dr. Nancy T. Ammerman
Dr. Sarah Frances Anders
*Anti-Defamation League
*Baptist Joint Committee
*General Board of Baptist State
    Convention of North
    Carolina
John F. Baugh
Dr. B. Bert Beach
The Rev. Dr. John Leland Berg
The Rev. Charles Bergstrom
Rabbi Louis Bernstein
The Rev. John Buchanan
Scott Bunton
The Rev. John Burns
The Rev. Dr. Joan Brown
    Campbell
The Rev. Dr. Tony Campolo
Jerome Chanes
Dr. Harvey Cox
The Rev. Dr. Calvin Didier
Edd Doerr
Bishop R. Sheldon Duecker
The Rev. Dr. James M. Dunn
The Rev. Dr. William R. Estep
The Rev. Dr. David Albert Farmer
The Rev. Dr. Ronald B. Flowers
Richard T. Foltin
Rabbi Lori Forman
Steven M. Freeman

Bishop Edwin R. Garrison
Dr. Edwin S. Gaustad
Dr. Alan Geyer
The Rev. Elenora Giddings Ivory
Rabbi Joseph B. Glaser
Rabbi Alfred Gottschalk
Leonard Greenberg
Phyllis Greenberg
Rabbi Leonard Guttman
James A. Hamilton
Dr. Robert T. Handy
The Rev. Dr. Walter Harrelson
The Rev. Dr. Stan Hastey
The Rev. Dr. E. Glenn Hinson
The Rev. Dr. Clint Hopkins
Richard Ice
Dr. Gregg Ivers
The Rev. Dr. Dan Ivins
Norman Jameson
The Rev. R. Mark Jordon
The Rev. Dean M. Kelley
The Rev. Dr. Thomas Kilgore, Jr.
John Klingenstein
The Rev. Leon Lawton
Norman Lear
The Rev. Dr. Bill J. Leonard
Charles Levendosky
The Rev. Dr. Dean H. Lewis
Rabbi Mordechai Liebling
Robert Lipshutz
The Rev. Barry Lynn
The Rev. Dr. Henry J. Lyons
The Rev. Dr. Robert L. Maddox
The Rev. Dr. Dean Majette
Rabbi Joel H. Meyers
Alfred H. Moses
The Rev. Dr. James A. Nash

*National Council of Churches of
Christ in the U.S.A.
*National Jewish Community
Relations Advisory Council
The Rev. Dr. Alan Neely
*People for the American Way
The Rev. Troy W. Petty
Dr. Richard Pierard
Samuel Rabinove
The Rev. Dr. Robert Rainwater
The Rev. J. George Reed
The Rev. Dr. John E. Roberts
Dr. Gary M. Ross
Rabbi A. James Rudin
Rabbi David Saperstein
The Rev. Dr. David Sapp
Rabbi Alexander Schindler
The Rev. Dr. Cecil Sherman
The Rev. Paul H. Sherry
Donald W. Shriver, Jr.
Peggy L. Shriver

Carroll D. Stevens
Rabbi Alan Silverstein
The Rev. Dr. Wallace Charles
Smith
The Rev. Dr. Gordon L. Sommers
The Right Rev. R. L. Speaks
Marc D. Stern
Phil D. Strickland
The Rev. Dr. John Swomley
Bishop Melvin G. Talbert
Rabbi David A. Teutsch
The Rev. Oliver S. Thomas
The Rev. Robert W. Tiller
Earl Trent
The Rev. Dr. Tim Turnham
The Rev. J. Brent Walker
The Rev. Dr. Daniel E. Weiss
The Rev. Bill Wilson
The Rev. Dr. Phillip Wogaman
The Rev. Aidsand Wright-Riggins
*Signatory organizations

James M. Dunn (right) introduces the "Shared Vision" statement after presenting it to Vice President Al Gore. Also addressing the statement was Rabbi A. James Rudin (left) of the American Jewish Committee.

Appendix E
Religion in the Public Schools
A Joint Statement of Current Law

The Constitution permits much private religious activity in and about the public schools. Unfortunately, this aspect of constitutional law is not as well known as it should be. Some say that the Supreme Court has declared the public schools "religion-free zones" or that the law is so murky that school officials cannot know what is legally permissible. The former claim is simply wrong. And as to the latter, while there are some difficult issues, much has been settled. It is also unfortunately true that public school officials, due to their busy schedules, may not be as fully aware of this body of law as they could be. As a result, in some school districts some of these rights are not being observed.

The organizations whose names appear below span the ideological, religious, and political spectrum. They nevertheless share a commitment both to the freedom of religious practice and to the separation of church and state such freedom requires. In that spirit, we offer this statement of consensus on current law as an aid to parents, educators, and students.

Many of the organizations listed below are actively involved in litigation about religion in the schools. On some of the issues discussed in this summary, some of the organizations have urged the courts to reach positions different than they did. Though there are signatories on both sides which have and will press for different constitutional treatments of some of the topics discussed below, they all agree that the following is an accurate statement of what the law currently is.

Student Prayers

(1) Students have the right to pray individually or in groups or to discuss their religious views with their peers so long as they are not disruptive. Because the establishment clause does not apply to purely private speech, students enjoy the right to read their Bibles or other scriptures, say grace before meals, pray before tests, and discuss religion with other willing student listeners. In the classroom students have the right to pray quietly except when required to be actively engaged in school activities (e.g., students may not decide to pray just as a teacher calls on them). In informal settings, such as the cafeteria or in the halls, students may pray either audibly or silently, subject to the same rules of order as apply to other speech in these locations. However, the right to engage in voluntary prayer does not include, for example, the right to have a captive audience listen or to compel other students to participate.

Graduation Prayer and Baccalaureates

(2) School officials may not mandate or organize prayer at graduation, nor may they organize a religious baccalaureate ceremony. If the school generally rents out its facilities to private groups, it must rent them out on the same terms, and on a first-come first-served basis, to organizers of privately sponsored religious baccalaureate services, provided that the school does not extend preferential treatment to the baccalaureate ceremony and the school disclaims official endorsement of the program.

(3) The courts have reached conflicting conclusions under the federal Constitution on student-initiated prayer at graduation. Until the issue is authoritatively resolved, schools should ask their lawyers what rules apply in their area.

Official Participation or Encouragement of Religious Activity

(4) Teachers and school administrators, when acting in those capacities, are representatives of the state, and, in those capacities, are themselves prohibited from encouraging or soliciting student religious or anti-religious activity. Similarly, when acting in their official capacities, teachers may not engage in religious activities with their students. However, teachers may engage in private religious activity in faculty lounges.

Teaching about Religion

(5) Students may be taught about religion, but public schools may not teach religion. As the U.S. Supreme Court has repeatedly said, "It might well be said that one's education is not complete without a study of comparative religion, or the history of religion and its relationship to the advancement of civilization." It would be difficult to teach art, music, literature, and most social studies without considering religious influences. The history of religion, comparative religion, the Bible (or other scripture)-as-literature (either as a separate course or within some other existing course) are all permissible public school subjects. It is both permissible and desirable to teach objectively about the role of religion in the history of the United States and other countries. One can teach that the Pilgrims came to this country with a particular religious vision; that Catholics and others have been subject to persecution; or that many of those participating in the abolitionist, women's suffrage, and civil rights movements had religious motivations.

(6) These same rules apply to the recurring controversy surrounding theories of evolution. Schools may teach about explanations of life on

earth, including religious ones (such as "creationism"), in comparative religion or social studies classes. In science class, however, they may present only genuinely scientific critiques of, or evidence for, any explanation of life on earth, but not religious critiques (beliefs unverifiable by scientific methodology). Schools may not refuse to teach evolutionary theory in order to avoid giving offense to religion, nor may they circumvent these rules by labeling as science an article of religious faith. Public schools must not teach as scientific fact or theory any religious doctrine, including "creationism," although any genuinely scientific evidence for or against any explanation of life may be taught. Just as they may neither advance nor inhibit any religious doctrine, teachers should not ridicule, for example, a student's religious explanation for life on earth.

Student Assignments and Religion

(7) Students may express their religious beliefs in the form of reports, homework, and artwork; and such expressions are constitutionally protected. Teachers may not reject or correct such submissions simply because they include a religious symbol or address religious themes. Likewise, teachers may not require students to modify, include, or excise religious views in their assignments, if germane. These assignments should be judged by ordinary academic standards of substance, relevance, appearance, and grammar.

(8) Somewhat more problematic from a legal point of view are other public expressions of religious views in the classroom. Unfortunately for school officials, there are traps on either side of this issue, and it is possible that litigation will result no matter what course is taken. It is easier to describe the settled cases than to state clear rules of law. Schools must carefully steer between the claims of student speakers who assert a right to express themselves on religious subjects and the asserted rights of student listeners to be free of unwelcome religious persuasion in a public school classroom.

a. Religious or anti-religious remarks made in the ordinary course of classroom discussion or student presentations are permissible and constitute a protected right. If in a sex education class a student remarks that abortion should be illegal because God has prohibited it, a teacher should not silence the remark, ridicule it, rule it out of bounds, or endorse it, any more than a teacher may silence a student's religiously-based comment in favor of choice.

b. If a class assignment calls for an oral presentation on a subject of the student's choosing, and, for example, the student responds by conducting a religious service, the school has the right—as well as the duty—to prevent itself from being used as a church. Other students are not voluntarily in attendance and cannot be forced to become an unwilling congregation.

c. Teachers may rule out of order religious remarks that are irrelevant to the subject at hand. In a discussion of Hamlet's sanity, for example, a student may not interject views on creationism.

Distribution of Religious Literature

(9) Students have the right to distribute religious literature to their schoolmates, subject to those reasonable time, place, and manner or other constitutionally acceptable restrictions imposed on the distribution of all non-school literature. Thus, a school may confine distribution of all literature to a particular table at particular times. It may not single out religious literature for burdensome regulation.

(10) Outsiders may not be given access to the classroom to distribute religious or anti-religious literature. No court has yet considered whether, if all other community groups are permitted to distribute literature in common areas of public schools, religious groups must be allowed to do so on equal terms subject to reasonable time, place, and manner restrictions.

"See You at the Pole"

(11) Student participation in before- or after-school events, such as "see you at the pole," is permissible. School officials, acting in an official capacity, may neither discourage nor encourage participation in such an event.

Religious Persuasion Versus Religious Harassment

(12) Students have the right to speak to, and attempt to persuade, their peers about religious topics just as they do with regard to political topics. But school officials should intercede to stop student religious speech if it turns into religious harassment aimed at a student or a small group of students. While it is constitutionally permissible for a student to approach another and issue an invitation to attend church, repeated invitations in the face of a request to stop constitute harassment. Where

this line is to be drawn in particular cases will depend on the age of the students and other circumstances.

Equal Access Act

(13) Student religious clubs in secondary schools must be permitted to meet and to have equal access to campus media to announce their meetings, if a school receives federal funds and permits any student noncurricular club to meet during noninstructional time. This is the command of the Equal Access Act. A noncurricular club is any club not related directly to a subject taught or soon-to-be taught in the school. Although schools have the right to ban all noncurriculum clubs, they may not dodge the law's requirement by the expedient of declaring all clubs curriculum-related. On the other hand, teachers may not actively participate in club activities, and "nonschool persons" may not control or regularly attend club meetings.

The act's constitutionality has been upheld by the Supreme Court rejecting claims that the act violates the establishment clause. The act's requirements are described in more detail in *The Equal Access Act and the Public Schools: Questions and Answers on the Equal Access Act,* a pamphlet published by a broad spectrum of religious and civil liberties groups.

Religious Holidays

(14) Generally, public schools may teach about religious holidays, and may celebrate the secular aspects of the holiday and objectively teach about their religious aspects. They may not observe the holidays as religious events. Schools should generally excuse students who do not wish to participate in holiday events. Those interested in further details should see *Religious Holidays in the Public Schools: Questions and Answers,* a pamphlet published by a broad spectrum of religious and civil liberties groups.

Excusal from Religiously Objectionable Lessons

(15) Schools enjoy substantial discretion to excuse individual students from lessons which are objectionable to that student or to his or her parent on the basis of religion. Schools can exercise that authority in ways which would defuse many conflicts over curriculum content. If it is proved that particular lessons substantially burden a student's free exercise of religion, and if the school cannot prove a compelling interest in requiring attendance, the school would be legally required to excuse the student.

Teaching Values

(16) Schools may teach civic virtues, including honesty, good citizenship, sportsmanship, courage, respect for the rights and freedoms of others, respect for persons and their property, civility, the dual virtues of moral conviction and tolerance and hard work. Subject to whatever rights of excusal exist (see 15 above) under the federal Constitution and state law, schools may teach sexual abstinence and contraception; whether and how schools teach these sensitive subjects is a matter of educational policy. However, these may not be taught as religious tenets. The mere fact that most, if not all, religions also teach these values does not make it unlawful to teach them.

Student Garb

(17) Religious messages on T-shirts and the like may not be singled out for suppression. Students may wear religious attire, such as yarmulkes and head scarves, and they may not be forced to wear gym clothes that they regard, on religious grounds, as immodest.

Released Time

(18) Schools have the discretion to dismiss students to off-premises religious instruction, provided that schools do not encourage or discourage participation or penalize those who do not attend. Schools may not allow religious instruction by outsiders on premises during the school day.

Endorsing Organizations

American Civil Liberties Union
American Ethical Union
American Humanist Association
American Jewish Committee
American Jewish Congress
American Muslim Council
Americans for Religious Liberty
Americans United for Separation of Church and State
Anti-Defamation League
Baptist Joint Committee
B'nai B'rith International
Christian Legal Society
Christian Science Church
Church of the Brethren, Washington Office
Church of Scientology International
Evangelical Lutheran Church in America,
    Lutheran Office for Governmental Affairs
Federation of Reconstructionist Congregations and Havurot
Friends Committee on National Legislation
General Conference of Seventh-day Adventists
Guru Gobind Singh Foundation
Hadassah, The Women's Zionist Organization of America
Interfaith Alliance
Interfaith Impact for Justice and Peace
National Association of Evangelicals
National Council of Churches
National Council of Jewish Women
National Jewish Community Relations Advisory Council (NJCRAC)
National Ministries, American Baptist Churches, USA
National Sikh Center
North American Council for Muslim Women
People for the American Way
Presbyterian Church (USA)
Reorganized Church of Jesus Christ of Latter Day Saints
Union of American Hebrew Congregations
Unitarian Universalist Association of Congregations
United Church of Christ, Office for Church in Society

Director of Information Services W. Barry Garrett, Executive Director C. Emanuel Carlson, Director of Research Services John W. Baker, and Director of Correlation Services James M. Sapp look at minutes from the agency's March 1970 meeting.

BJC staff in 1981 included (from left) Director of Information Services Stan Hastey, Director of Denominational Relations Victor Tupitza, Director of Research and General Counsel John W. Baker, and Executive Director James M. Dunn.

BJC General Counsel J. Brent Walker opposes proposed school prayer amendment at an interfaith press conference, November 1994.